Find Fish
Anywhere, Anytime

Find Fish Anywhere, Anytime

Complete Angler's Library®
North American Fishing Club
Minneapolis, Minnesota

Find Fish Anywhere, Anytime

Copyright © 1991, North American Fishing Club

Library of Congress Catalog Card Number 91-61686
ISBN 0-914697-39-0

Printed in U.S.A.
10 11 12 13 14 15 16

Contents

Acknowledgments

The North American Fishing Club would like to thank everyone who helped with the creation of this book.

Wildlife artist Virgil Beck created the cover art; artists David Rottinghaus and John A. (Buzz) Buczynski created illustrations. Co-author Mark Strand provided some of the photographs throughout the book. Outdoor photographers C. Boyd Pfeiffer, Dale Spartas and Soc Clay contributed additional photos.

A special thanks to Joseph Bates, Jr.'s widow, Helen Ellis Bates, and his daughter, Pamela Bates Richards, for all their help and cooperation in reprinting his works in this fine book.

Thanks to the Fishing Club's publication staff for their efforts: Editor and Publisher Mark LaBarbera, Managing Editor Steve Pennaz, Managing Editor of Books Ron Larsen, Editorial Assistant Colleen Ferguson and Layout Artist Dean Peters. Thanks also to Vice President of Product Marketing Mike Vail, Marketing Manager Cal Franklin and Marketing Project Coordinator Laura Resnik.

About The Authors

Joseph D. Bates, Jr. (1903 - 1988) has written 16 books on the sport of fishing, ranging from teaching novices and youngsters "how to fish" to his international authority books such as *Streamer Fly Tying and Fishing* and *Atlantic Salmon Flies and Fishing*.

He was known around the world as "the fisherman's fisherman." He has taught more people, young and old, the wonderful sport of fishing in all its aspects—art, skill and joy. Much of *Find Fish Anywhere, Anytime* is an updated version of Bates' 1974 book *How To Find Fish And Make Them Strike*. It is his family's hope that Bates' expertise and knowledge of fishing would be passed on to generations and kept alive. This book will help do just that.

Bates was born in West Springfield, Massachusetts. He was educated at the Massachusetts Institute of Technology and then joined his father's advertising agency, Snow, Bates and Orme, Inc., where he became vice president. At the same time, he became an officer in the 104th Infantry, Massachusetts National Guard that later would award him with the Long Service Medal for 27 years of service.

During World War II, he served in the South Pacific—Australia, New Guinea and the Philippines. He was awarded three battle stars on his Philippine Liberation Medal

and was promoted to Lieutenant Colonel.

After World War II, Bates became a public relations consultant for several large corporations which included Colgate-Palmolive, Nestle, Alcoa and several fishing tackle firms. While consulting, he began to write for various magazines on different fishing subjects and eventually began to author his own books on angling. In 1946, the Bates agency had to create advertisements for a new type of fishing tackle: spinning rods and reels. This tackle had been introduced in the 1930s with little success. Bates helped to popularize the technique of spinning in the United States. His first book was entitled *Spinning for American Game Fish.*

Bates is also known as the authority on the history and effectiveness of Atlantic salmon flies. Many of his books are now considered to be collectors' items.

Mark Strand strongly believes that there is a set of skills anglers can master that will help them find virtually any species of fish, in any type of water.

4

"If you can learn to read lake maps, and use sonar," he says, "that's a start. If you can also learn to gather information off the water and fish efficiently once you're on it, fishing doesn't seem to be such a mystery anymore."

Mark's work may be familiar to many NAFC members. He is the author of *Walleye Tactics, Tips & Tales*, another book in the Complete Angler's Library series, as well as numerous magazine articles in *North American Fisherman* magazine.

Mark belongs to the Outdoor Writers Association of America and the Association of Great Lakes Outdoor Writers. He is a full-time free-lance writer and photographer with a journalism degree from the University of Minnesota, where he minored in fisheries and wildlife science. He worked as a researcher for the *Hunting & Fishing Library*, and as a writer and photographer for Babe Winkelman Productions before going on his own.

Mark began fishing when he was three years old. His family was known as an "outdoors" family and spent all weekends and vacations hunting and fishing. "When you're introduced to fishing that young," he says, "you will either love or hate it—I

love it." Mark has fished throughout the heart of America—all around the Great Lakes, Washington, Oregon, California, Arizona, Arkansas, Texas and Florida. He has also fished the western and central parts of Canada, as well as near the Arctic Circle.

Other than fishing and hunting, Mark's special interests include reading fiction and environmental issues, training his dog, running and weight training. He also loves outdoor writing and photography, which is why he does it full time. "It's nice to get up in the morning and do something that you are interested in," he says. "That's what I consider success."

Mark has a healthy respect for the fishing pioneers, such as Joe Bates. "The early fishermen were really good," Mark says, "especially when you consider all the things they did *not* have, such as lake maps and sonar units. It's a wonderful thing that we can enjoy the wisdom of a great angler and writer like Joseph D. Bates, Jr., and sprinkle in a few words about the advances that let us take his teachings and adapt them to all the gadgets we now carry with us."

Mark resides in Andover, Minnesota with his wife Jeanne and their son William.

Foreword

Masters Walleye Circuit tournament pro Mike McClelland hit the nail on the head when he said, "You can't catch a fish that isn't there." And, although McClelland is best known for his uncanny ability in catching walleyes, what he says holds true for whatever species you pursue whether it's bass, crappie, catfish, trout, pike or any other finned creature that inhabits our lakes and streams.

Yet, the majority of today's anglers refuse to believe the key to catching more fish is simply fishing where there are fish. Many still believe in the so-called "magic bait" and consider it the most direct line to a full stringer. Other, slightly more enlightened anglers, realizing there is no such thing as a magic bait, spend countless hours working to improve their presentations and angling skills, only to become frustrated when their catch rates don't improve dramatically. The best anglers, those who consistently catch fish under a variety of conditions, also work to improve their presentations, but they also use whatever means available to help them pinpoint exact fish locations.

There are shortcuts to finding fish. Some are very simple to employ, while others can be relatively involved. But, all of them work, and it is to your advantage to add them to your bag of fishing skills.

Find Fish Anywhere, Anytime will help you become a better angler because it will help you improve your ability to find fish under many different conditions. And while there are other books on this topic out there, *Find Fish Anywhere, Anytime* is unique in that the two authors share their expertise in finding fish when many can't. Joe Bates, an acknowledged trout fishing expert, will help you analyze various waters. While the specific application is often for trout, the principles that he applies are applicable to a number of species. In chapters 8 and 9, for example, Bates takes NAFC members through the thought process used in deciding what situations look most promising for catching fish. In addition, co-author Mark Strand shares some of his secrets for locating fish quickly, even on unfamiliar waters, as well as talking about effective use of electronics and maps in preparing yourself to take fish.

Much of the angler's success depends upon how well he or she learns to "read water" and to anticipate where the fish are and what they're doing. While the book does touch upon various lures and baits, the emphasis is on how to quickly locate and get into position to take fish. In most cases, the little tricks these men use to locate fish will help you, no matter where or what you fish.

I hope you enjoy *Find Fish Anywhere, Anytime*.

Steve Pennaz
Executive Director
North American Fishing Club

Preface

While the science of fishing has undergone rapid, techno-
logical change in recent years, a lot of the basics that
have been learned through experience and passed on from one
fisherman to another have not.

This book is representative of what has happened in fishing
over the past generation. It seeks to meld those basics with the
advances in technology, particularly in the use of electronic
fishfinders and new or refined techniques for narrowing the
selections in picking likely spots where fish hang out.

Co-author Joseph Bates, Jr., developed his expertise in fish
finding in the pre-electronic era. He had few peers in being able
to see fish where others could not. Having been an ardent trout
fisherman, Bates became expert at finding fish particularly in
shallow water situations. Co-author Mark Strand is a product of
the burgeoning electronics in fishing era and has considerable
knowledge about the science of finding fish with sonar devices.

However, electronic devices are only a part of the tools of
the trade. It's often said that an angler has to learn to "think
like a fish" in order to catch fish consistently. It's probably not
so much thinking like a fish (for even fisheries biologists may
have difficulty doing that) as it is developing the ability to
really "read water" as our authors will help you do. There are

tip-offs, or signs as to what is happening beneath the surface if we have the ability to recognize them and act upon them. Expert fishermen develop the ability to "see" the world beneath the surface, utilizing all the information that is available to them. When you learn to do this, your success rate will improve dramatically. Fishing will be more fun, too.

Unfortunately, we no longer have the advantage of Mr. Bates' counsel except through his writings. We are sure you will agree, however, that his skill in teaching anglers how to find fish is on a par with his skill in fishing.

Ron Larsen
Managing Editor
Complete Angler's Library

Basics of
Finding Fish

1

Understanding Fish Habits

There is a saying that "10 percent of the fishermen catch 90 percent of the fish." Although this statement has never been verified, a germ of truth is lodged in the assertion. A large percentage of anglers often come home fishless and most of them have one thing in common: slight knowledge of their quarry's habits. The purpose of this book is to enlarge that knowledge and to help NAFC members join that "10 percent" who catch most of the fish most of the time.

To catch fish, we first have to find them. This is where we begin our study. Anglers generally go about finding fish in one of four ways: location, eyesight, reading the water and using electronics.

Location

Those who fish an area often are more apt to learn the choicest locations, such as the quietly flowing water behind a certain rock, the dark current by an undercut bank or the sanctuary of submerged roots below a dead tree. These places remain good because new fish move into them after others have been caught. The trouble with this method is the angler is at a disadvantage when fishing new territory.

Eyesight

Another method is fishing by eyesight. Though this can be

Half the battle in catching fish is finding them. Even some of the standby "honeyholes" can let fishermen down, but it's particularly difficult with "new lakes" like this recently developed reservoir.

Understanding Fish Habits 13

done while wading, or while sitting in a slow-moving boat, it is best done by remaining in one place and observing the water. You may see a feeding fish rise from behind a midstream rock, or the slight dimple it makes when sucking in an insect. Since the fish occupies a certain lie, into which it periodically settles, it may come up from this position again and again.

In eyesight fishing, you look for faint signs of fish—a shape near the bottom, or a slight movement as a fish alters its position. You may notice a slight swirl, a head-and-tail rise, a tailing only, or some similar indication of feeding fish. To the expert, various types of rises not only indicate the presence of fish, but also what they are feeding on, as you shall learn later. On lakes and ponds, the flurry of small baitfish breaking the surface tells you that gamefish are feeding from below. Tiny dimples in a windrow or wind edge tell you gamefish (or baitfish) are sipping insects on the surface. Unusual motion in lily pads indicates that bass are feeding in the shallows. These are only a few examples.

Some anglers become adept at eyesight fishing, while others think the faint signs of gamefish mean nothing. The ability to perceive fish is acquired by experience; it comes easier to some people than to others. Try to develop this ability, because it can be combined with other methods of finding fish.

Reading The Water
The third method is the ability to "read the water." It is the best one because it can be applied anywhere. Future chapters in this book will develop this method as it applies to various species in lakes or streams. Reading the water is the ability to instinctively select the few good locations from the many poor or fishless ones. It is the ability to "think like a fish," knowing the hiding places that the fish themselves seek.

Electronics
The fourth, and last, method is by using fishfinding sonar and navigational aids. Many fish live near mid-lake structure or suspend near baitfish, and would be hard to locate without sonar because there are no visible signs of their presence. With sonar units, it is possible to "see" the fish and determine their exact depth. Once you locate these fish, you can return to them

Stream Flow Across A Stream Bed

FASTER
FLOW

FASTER
FLOW

MODERATE FLOW

Obstructions in a stream create areas of moderate flow which fish prefer to inhabit. Moderate to slow current flows along the sides and bottom of a stream; the surface current is also slower than the middle. The current is always moderate behind a midstream rock.

again and again with a location principle called Loran-C, which uses land-based radio stations to electronically "triangulate" exact positions on the water.

During my apprentice years as a beginner in angling, I was fortunate to have been included on various fishing trips with great anglers. Many of these anglers were older and had obtained by experience an uncanny ability to read the water. All of them took time to "read the water" before they fished it, and to plan the strategy of their approach before making the first cast.

I remember one youthful day when Herbie Welch, an angling crony of President Herbert Hoover, took me fishing on the Kennebago stream in Maine. After arriving at one of the best pools, I promptly waded in and started casting. Herbie, on the other hand, remained sitting on the bank, quietly smoking his pipe. Because the slight frown on his face indicated I must be doing something wrong, I waded ashore and joined him.

"Aren't you going to fish?" I asked.

"Now, you sit right down here and let me tell you a thing or two," he said. "You waded into the best part of the run and scared the fish there. You should have seen them scooting away. Before you start to fish a new spot, you should take time to study the water. Sit down and relax and look it over. You waded too close to that rock before fishing it, and I saw a good trout feeding there before you splashed in. Over there is another run you may not have disturbed. You can reach that lush green area on the far bank, where a spring trickles in—a real hotspot in the summer."

Herbie went on to explain how to read the water of the pool to select the good spots from the others. He pointed to where he would wade to cast, and how the fly should be fished in each spot. He explained the sequence of casting position—where to start fishing the pool, and what to do next, and so on after that. From that time on, we would stand or sit together in new places while I outlined the strategy of fishing them. He would correct me when I was wrong, and explain what I had missed. He taught me much about how to read the water—lessons never to be forgotten. We frequently would stroll along the bank to examine the stream and to plan how we would fish it. This disclosed depressions, submerged rocks and feeding lanes which we might not have observed while fishing. Then, we would return later and fly cast when the stream was undisturbed.

Of course, all anglers can read the water to some extent. The best ones have learned by study and experience. In the next few chapters, photographs of actual situations are shown so you can study them and gain important experience without wasting time while fishing.

Locating Fish By Their Habits

Because fish don't resemble people, are cold-blooded and live in water, most anglers don't realize their requirements are more like those of people than anglers might think. When considering the requirements of fish and relating them to the water, you can come close to locating them by their habits.

While each species varies somewhat in its requirements, there are five basic ones, plus the inborn urge to travel (usually once a year) to a suitable place to spawn. Fish need sufficient oxygen in water where they live. They want this water to be in a comfortable temperature range. They usually want a place to hide or rest which gives them adequate protection. Those in streams or other fast-flow areas seek places of moderate flow where they can rest in reasonable comfort without combating currents. Finally, of course, they want abundant food nearby, or at least convenient enough so that they can travel to it with a minimum amount of effort.

When considering these five basic location requirements, you can eliminate certain areas or water levels, and concentrate on the places where these five requirements are met. There are several fine points to all this which will be explored later, but first let's define the requirements more exactly.

Sufficient Oxygen

Fish need oxygen to breathe just as humans do. Oxygen is dissolved in water and then taken from it by action of the fish's gills. People who live near sea level aren't comfortable at high altitudes because the air contains less oxygen. Because some fish species require more oxygen than others, you should seek them in areas containing more oxygen rather than less. In reservoirs, water fountains jet up so the water can absorb oxygen from the air. Streams, waterfalls or turbulence accomplish this naturally. On the other hand, pollution from industrial waste, sewage and such contaminants as sawdust from lumber mills reduce the oxygen content of water, often to such an extent that gamefish can't live in it. Decaying vegetation, often found in man-made impoundments and beaver ponds, may temporarily have this effect.

Suitable Temperature Range

Most people like temperatures in the 70-degree range. When the air becomes too cold or too hot, some move to where it is warmer or cooler. Fish are even more particular about water temperature, being sensitive to changes as small as even a fraction of a degree. Each species seeks its ideal temperature, but can tolerate a somewhat wider range, as the temperature-activity table for freshwater fish on page 19 indicates. A temperature-activity table for trout is included on page 223, and similar tables can be worked out for other species.

Fish can exist, if they have to, in water well out of their optimum (ideal) or tolerant temperature ranges, but they become more or less dormant in these uncomfortable temperatures and often won't even take a bait that is drifting in front of their noses.

This indicates you should consider water temperatures and seek fish in the areas or depths where ideal or tolerant temperatures exist. In the summer, bass come into the shallows to feed between dusk and daylight when the water is cooler. However, they often seek adjoining deeper water during midday when surface water is too warm.

Since suitable water temperature is important when trying to find fish, it will be dealt with to a greater extent in Chapter 3. Modern sonar, which also is discussed in greater detail in Chapter 5, actually shows depths at which suitable temperatures exist. The object is to determine these depths and get bait or lures down there. Usually, these depths intersect the sides of lakes, or submerged reefs or islands. In streams where exposed areas are too warm, fish either lie deep in the cooler water of pools, or migrate to water with more acceptable cold-water temperatures.

Adequate Protection

Gamefish, except perhaps some of the anadromous species (like salmon) that leave deep water to return to rivers of origin to spawn, have learned by instinct they must hide from fishermen and predators if they are to survive. They venture from cover in search of food when they think they will be undisturbed, but remain under cover, or quickly return to it, when danger threatens. In streams, such protective cover may be the overhang of a rock in the current, the area under a ledge or a fallen tree, an undercut bank, or the depths of a pool. In lakes and ponds, it may be the shady cover of lily pads or the concealment of other vegetation, submerged roots or brush piles, rocks or the depth of the water itself.

Anglers learn to identify such places instinctively and they know when such places also satisfy other requirements being

Complete Angler's Library

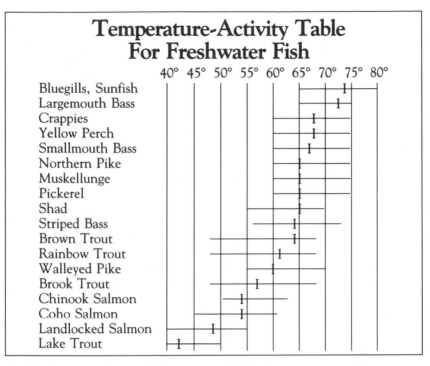

Temperature-Activity Table
For Freshwater Fish

	40°	45°	50°	55°	60°	65°	70°	75°	80°
Bluegills, Sunfish								I	
Largemouth Bass								I	
Crappies							I		
Yellow Perch							I		
Smallmouth Bass							I		
Northern Pike						I			
Muskellunge						I			
Pickerel						I			
Shad						I			
Striped Bass					I				
Brown Trout					I				
Rainbow Trout				I					
Walleyed Pike				I					
Brook Trout			I						
Chinook Salmon		I							
Coho Salmon		I							
Landlocked Salmon	I								
Lake Trout	I								

On this chart, "I" indicates ideal temperature. While this may vary somewhat in various regions, this chart should be followed unless regional data suggests variation. The horizontal line indicates optimum temperature range. Fish usually will not take lures well outside of this range. Members of the pike family, which include northern pike, muskellunge and the various pickerels, are much less fussy about water temperatures than other species. While the range shown for them is the optimum one, they usually will take lures when the water is slightly warmer or very much colder.

discussed, they are almost certain to conceal gamefish. Anadromous species, such as salmon, shad and steelhead, which spend most of their lives in the ocean or deep freshwater lakes, often lie or cruise in sight, unmindful that anglers are plainly visible and are fishing for them.

Of course, the instinct of concealment, of hiding from the eyes of predators, is more acute in some species of fish than others. Members of the trout families are particularly shy, usually fleeing for protection even when they see the flash of a rod being handled by an unseen angler. Gamefish do not always run for cover when danger threatens, but they usually will not feed and will ignore anglers' lures.

Anglers know gamefish flee from the sound, as well as from the sight, if a man is on the bank or in the water. You may spot fish while walking clumsily along a streambank or when noisily handling equipment in a boat, but you won't catch them. Sound waves carry long distances underwater, and fish are quick to distinguish unnatural vibrations from natural ones.

Reasonable Comfort

Another similarity between the requirements of fish and people is their desire for comfort. Most people dislike strong winds, so they try to stand or walk where they are protected. Fish dislike combating strong current, so they rest in areas of moderate or broken flow.

What is moderate flow? An easy way to determine the difference between fast and moderate flow is to stand facing downstream in the fast water of a river. Put your hand in the water on either side of your boot and you'll notice the flow of water will be equal in strength to the current. Put your hand in front of or directly behind the boot, however, and you will find the flow is more moderate. Any major obstruction in a stream, such as a rock, the trunk of a fallen tree, or a jutting ledge, produces the same effect, but usually to a much greater degree. The obstruction creates an area of moderate flow in which fish like to rest; they can lie in such places with a minimum of exertion. These places are often called holding positions.

While doing the boot experiment, look downward where the boot's obstruction causes moderate flow, and beside the boot, where it doesn't. You will see two streaming lines in the water on each side of the moderate flow area where they meet the fast unimpeded flow. These are called edges. You can see them on both sides of a rock or a ledge in a stream, where a brook enters a river, currents converge downstream of an island and in other places that we'll discuss later.

Fish like to lie inside these edges, where there is moderate flow. They look toward the faster water for food, and will flash out to take it, but they quickly return to their holding positions inside the edge in the moderate flow where they can remain in position without undue exertion. Because obstructions in a stream cause areas of moderate flow, it is obvious that streams flow more slowly close to their banks or beds. Rocks and gravel, tree roots, vegetation and other such impediments break the current to send the faster flow away from the banks. The

Complete Angler's Library

Fish congregate along food lanes, and so do birds. These gulls tell an angler that there are baitfish and probably gamefish along those rocks.

slowest flow is along the streambed and the more moderate flow along its sides. Surface water also tends to flow slower than the main current.

This is one reason why gamefish usually lie along the bottom of a stream or along its sides. Another is that protection and food are available in such places. The side that is in the shade is usually the best one for fishing.

Abundant Food

Gamefish congregate where food is easiest to find, or they travel to such places from their havens of security when they are hungry. In streams, the water-reading angler notices feed lanes—relatively narrow, faster currents which catch food and wash it downstream. Floating objects are a tip-off. When a feed lane goes past a rock or other obstructions offering moderate flow, thus offering protection, comfort and food, the place should be a hotspot. Feed lanes often pass by undercut banks or protruding ledges. Such places satisfy these requirements and thus should be hotspots, also. Active eddies may not offer much protection, except perhaps in deep water, but they may be cruising areas and feeding grounds for less spooky fish than trout—smallmouth bass, for example. Even trout go to such places at feeding times, mostly because schools of minnows can be found.

Trout periodically leave their protective havens to feed in the tails of pools or in riffles, usually around daylight or after dusk, or even under brighter conditions when hatches of insects are emerging. Since their protective havens are at a distance then, they are wary and scoot for cover at the slightest provocation. Except when trout are rising to insects or nymphs, most of their feeding will tend to occur on or near the bottom. In the deeper stretches of pools, the "in between" water is usually unproductive; yet this is the area where novices do most of their fishing.

Feeding habits of fish in ponds and lakes, where currents do not exist, create different problems. Since these have many facets, they will be discussed in detail in Chapters 4 and 7. Briefly, fish in ponds or lakes spend most of their time at levels where water temperatures suit them; usually, these temperature levels are near the sides of lakes, or islands, submerged reefs or ridges. From these places, they travel to feeding areas in shallower water—rocky shorelines, lily-pad areas or similar places abundant in grasses and other vegetation. Fish feed at regular intervals and their travels can often be predicted. The routes from the depths to the feeding areas are paths of migration chosen because of bottom contours which make such travel easier and safer. This gets into the interesting and valuable details of "structure fishing" to be discussed primarily in Chapters 4 and 7.

When these five requirements are considered together, the basic elements of finding fish can be better understood. By combining the five and pinpointing the best locations, an angler can eliminate the majority of areas which aren't productive. The "sufficient oxygen" requirement may not be

Spawning Information For Freshwater Fish

Species	Spawning Season	Approx. Water Temperature	Spawning Location
Bluegills Sunfish	Late May to early August	65°-70°	Sand and gravel areas with vegetation by pond and lake shorelines
Largemouth Bass	Early May to late June	62°-70° (north) 65°-80° (south)	Sand and gravel areas with vegetation by pond and lake shorelines
Crappies	Late May to late July	60°-70° (north) 70°-80° (south)	Sand and gravel areas with vegetation in water less than 10 feet deep
Yellow Perch	Mid-March to mid-May	45°-50°	Weedy or brushy areas in shallow to deep pond and lake water (Sometimes migrate up tributaries)
Smallmouth Bass	Late April to late June	59°-65°	Sand and gravel areas 5 to 20 feet deep in lakes, ponds and streams
Northern Pike	Early spring	35°-50°	Shallow, weedy lake areas (migrate up tributaries to flooded areas)
Muskellunge	April to June	48°-60°	Shallow lakes, bays in muddy, stumpy bottom
Pickerel	Early spring	45°-50°	Weedy shoal lake, pond or tributary stream areas
Shad	November (south) to June (far north)	55°-70°	Upper river reaches with free access to ocean
Brown Trout	October to February	50°-65°	Tributary streams or rocky shallow lake areas
Rainbow Trout	Spring	50°-65°	Tributary streams or rocky shallow lake areas
Walleyes	Spring, after ice breaks up	45°-50°	Shoal lake or tributary stream areas
Brook Trout	September to December	48°-55°	Small gravel brooks or gravel shorelines of lakes
Chinook Salmon	Nearly every month, depending on run type	50°-55°	Gravel upper reach areas of streams with free ocean access
Coho Salmon	October to February	50°-55°	Gravel upper reach areas of streams with free ocean access
Landlocked Salmon	Early October to late November	45°-55°	Lake inlets or outlets with gravel or rubble bottom
Lake Trout	Early October to late November	37°-50°	Gravel or rocky lake bottoms or reefs at varying depths

This is a generalized guideline for determining when your favorite species will be spawning. Geographical temperature variations prevent providing concise regional information. Consult local anglers for more accurate details about your favorite species. Also, be sure to check your local fishing regulations for limitations on taking species during spawning. Most rainbow trout spawn in the spring with the time varying because of regional climatic conditions. Steelhead (anadromous rainbow trout) normally ascend rivers to spawn between October and February, but some Pacific streams have summer runs.

Understanding Fish Habits

pertinent if the water is relatively free of pollution and appears to be well-oxygenated. The "reasonable comfort" doesn't apply unless water is flowing. Of the other three, a "suitable temperature range" is usually the most important because fish do more resting than feeding, and they rest where water temperatures are to their liking. When streams get too warm in the summer, fish select the depths of pools or they run up cold-water brooks. When the near-surface water of ponds and lakes becomes too warm or too cold, fish select depths where the water is more comfortable. Temperature gauges allow you to determine these depths.

The requirement of "abundant food" is also important, but anglers can learn how to tempt them to strike baits or lures. The requirement of "adequate protection" is always important except in certain cases where fish leave protective cover to find food. We now know that protective cover has two meanings—the cover of hiding places which offer concealment for fish in shallow water and the cover of depth in relatively deep water. When water temperatures are suitable, this depth may be near the surface if the water is murky, or much deeper if the water is clear. Fish seem to think they are safe when they can't see what's going on above the surface. Thus, anglers usually combine the requirements of water temperature and protective cover to find fish, preferably in areas offering an adequate or abundant food supply. This narrows the good fishing places down to a relative few.

Let's look at six stream situations which help to illustrate the requirements of protection, comfort and food in streams. These are given here because they are basic. Other interesting and more complex situations applying to streams and lakes will be given in future chapters.

Spawning Migrations

Earlier in this chapter another way of finding fish was noted—the fish's inborn urge to travel to a suitable place to spawn. The time of year varies among different species but you can locate them, often in great numbers, by understanding their spawning habits because they migrate in schools for this purpose. Here are a few examples:

In early spring, vast schools of yellow perch leave

Chesapeake Bay and migrate up tributary rivers to spawn. They do this when water temperatures reach about 45 degrees Fahrenheit in the fresh and flowing water of smaller river branches often only a few feet wide and a foot or two deep. Anglers who don't know this may fish in deeper water with little or no results. Anglers who recognize this fact meet the hoards of perch upriver and hook one on nearly every cast.

In New England, a red-letter fishing week occurs early in May when smelt, which have run up the tributary streams from lakes and bays to spawn, return to the lakes and bays again. Trout and landlocked salmon wait for them near the stream mouths and big ones can be caught there. Anglers who understand this spawning urge can feast on succulent fried smelt as well as enjoying the excellent fishing for trout and salmon.

The annual runs of anadromous fish from oceans or the Great Lakes to spawning rivers are well known to anglers. The fish are usually rainbow trout (steelhead) or the several species of salmon. These runs usually occur between late fall and early spring. Some streams also have summer runs. The introduction of exotic species, like skamania steelhead or coho salmon, are making year-round fisheries in areas like the Great Lakes. Anglers native to a certain river know exactly when the fish should be there and which pools should be most productive as the season advances. Lake trout also migrate from deep water into the shallows in lakes like the Great Lakes, giving anglers who know their habits greater opportunities.

Brook trout that live in lakes collect around the mouths of tributary streams in the fall waiting for the spawning urge to impel them upstream when the streams' flows and temperatures are to their liking. Brown trout sometimes do the same, but are less migratory. Rainbow trout that are not anadromous are spring spawners which often go up streams at that time. A bit of local research will let fishermen know what's going on so they can find pinpoint runs and enjoy prime fishing.

2

Senses Of Fish

inding fish is only part of the angling game. Enticing them to strike a natural bait or artificial lure is about the rest. This is when a knowledge of the fish's sensory equipment is helpful—how it responds to scent, sound and sight. Many anglers return home empty-handed simply because they frighten fish that would have struck or because they chose the wrong bait or lure for the situation.

The senses of mammals, birds and insects are far more finely tuned and developed than are those of humans, and so are the senses of fish. In their fascinating book on fish behavior, *Through the Fish's Eye*, co-authors Mark Sosin and John Clark state that two-hundredths of a drop of extract from a seal's skin can be detected by salmon in a 23,000-gallon swimming pool, or in a pool of the same size in a river. Tagged salmon smolts can travel thousands of miles in the ocean and return after years at sea to the same river and its tributary in which they were born. Those who underestimate the senses of fish, or fail to comprehend them pay the penalty of failing to catch them.

The Sense Of Sight

Some older angling books say fish are color-blind and see lures only in shades of gray. This isn't so because the retinal structure of fish is similar to that of humans.

For example, an experiment was conducted with panels of different colors in an aquarium of goldfish. The fish were taught

A low silhouette and a tan fishing vest helped this angler in taking a nice trout from this stream where the fish's viewpoint is very good.

in a matter of hours that they would be fed if they nosed the red panel, but that no food would result from nosing the others. Panels were shifted and colors were varied from intense to pale; yet, the fish always nosed the red or pink one to obtain food. This proves fish have acute sight and accurate color perception, although it varies slightly among species.

Knowledgeable anglers wear dull-colored clothing, avoiding bright colors and white in favor of tan, green and gray. Knowledgeable anglers also keep their silhouettes low over clear water because light refraction in water enables fish to see them. Unbelievers can walk slowly and quietly to streamside and watch fish scoot for cover. Thus, wading anglers have an advantage over bank fishermen—the deeper they wade, the lower their silhouette.

In doing research for this book, I tried to find authentic information about color selection of lures under various conditions. I talked or corresponded with many famous anglers, and read numerous books on fish behavior and angling. Many of the answers I got were contradictory, but I was able to find sufficient agreement to formulate a few theories of my own.

In surface or near-surface fishing, you should imitate food that fish are (or may be) feeding on. Thus, dry flies, wet flies and nymphs imitate the naturals in shape and color. Select streamers and bucktails that imitate the color, shape and size of prevalent baitfish. Minnow and frog imitation lures are selected the same way. However, questions pop up in other areas. When selecting an attractor pattern in streamer flies, should anglers choose yellow and red, white and blue, or something else? When selecting a lure, should anglers choose an all-black one or a red and white one, or should they try chartreuse with an orange belly or another of the dozens of color schemes provided by manufacturers? These decisions depend on the brightness of the day, the depth and clarity of the water and other factors.

Recall the colors of the spectrum, as seen in a rainbow. The red end of the spectrum has a long wavelength and low reflectance; that is, the colors at this end disappear more quickly, the deeper they are fished. This is because water is a poor conductor of light. In clear water, light doesn't penetrate much beyond 30 feet or so, and in cloudy water barely 10 feet. Thus, red and orange are visible near the surface but not in deep water. On the other hand, the colors at the blue end of the spectrum have short wavelengths and high reflectance, so these can be seen more clearly in deep water. A white disk or an anchor painted white can help you judge water clarity where you're planning to fish.

Now, look at the non-colors from black to white. Black, like red, has a long wavelength and low reflectance, while white is just the opposite. Shades of gray, like those of yellow, are in the middle range.

What does this prove? Not much. The important thing to remember is that short-wavelength, high-reflectance colors (the blues and greens) can be seen better by fish in deep water. The fluorescent and phosphorescent qualities of colored lures that are popular today appear to make these lures even more attractive to the fish. They seem to enhance the attractor qualities of short-wavelength, high-reflectance colors.

However, some experts don't agree with this in spite of scientific evidence. Many find, for example, that black lures are effective in deep water. Others use blue and white lures for deep fishing. Chartreuse, which is light green (green and white) with a little yellow, has long been a favorite color, as well as blue and purple. For deep saltwater jigging, many experts prefer white or green. Thus, the short-wave colors seem more popular than the long-wave ones for deep water.

On bright days in clear water, the best non-imitative fly is a light one with plenty of tinsel. This is because in sunlight the sides of baitfish are reflective and shimmer and shine as they twist and turn while gathering food. Lures should be silver, or another light, reflective color. However, this can be carried too far. A highly polished silver or nickel spoon, for example, can have too much flash in bright sunlight, and can spook fish.

On bright days in discolored water (or dull ones in clear water) fly and lure selection is in the middle range. Flies, generally, should be dull (gray) with less tinsel, usually only as a ribbing. Spoons and spinners should be less flashy, and plugs generally should be in middle-range colors. One practice is to let metal lures tarnish and to rub them with crocus cloth when needed for proper flash (reflectance). Tarnished ones rubbed to moderate flash are excellent under these conditions.

Another favorite practice in these situations is to use flies with a bit of fluorescence in them, usually as a butt. Other lures can have fluorescent beads. Fluorescence increases light reflection. Use of fluorescent lures is more effective on dull days or in discolored water. On dull days in discolored water, experience tells anglers that flies should be dark with no tinsel, lures dark with no flash, or else just a bit. This advice, in my mind, is sound, but by all means try bright colors if you're not catching fish. Let the fish determine the color.

All this depends on the actinic (radiant) value of light and its direction and influence on the water. When two or more persons are fishing together, one can fish by the rules while the others can experiment until they find the right lure.

Another widespread opinion is that dull flies are more effective in warm water (over 50 degrees) and brighter ones are better in colder water (under 50 degrees). This may apply to other lures, as well. In addition, most agree that large flies and lures are best in fast heavy water, medium-sized ones in normal flow and small ones in low water. This is merely a matter of using lures that fish can see easily.

Anglers who fish for brown trout and other species at night prefer lures that are black through gray to white. They prefer black or dark lures on dark nights, grayish lures during half-moon periods and white lures when the moon is about full. At night, some opt for dark lures all the time. During World War II, frogmen said the ships' hulls which were hardest to see from below were the white ones because their silhouettes were much more difficult to see. This is the reason for white (or very light) fly lines. Black or dark lines on the water are easily seen from below. Black is the "color" that reflects the least light; white reflects the most.

Finally, as far as color selection goes, the popular Dardevle spoon sells best in red and white, although it comes in many other color combinations. Red and white also are popular colors for other lures, such as chuggers and flies. Why? The two colors are entirely opposite in reflectance value so one is seen more clearly when the other is not, making the combination of more or less universal use.

The Sense Of Hearing

Although their acoustical organs are concealed, fish can hear sounds more acutely and over a wider range than humans. (Also, sound travels five times faster in water than it does in air.) Scientists say fish can hear nymphs crawling on rocks and will swim to the source of the sound to feed.

Anglers who noisily approach a stream usually find it "fishless." I recall a time after lunch on a wilderness stream in Maine when I was sitting on a small bluff, watching trout and baitfish in a pool. A big trout lying between the edges of a rock would rise periodically to pick insects from the surface. Several other trout were peacefully resting or feeding here and there, but I waited for cloudier conditions before starting the afternoon's fishing. Suddenly, the big trout disappeared under a ledge of the rock, and all the others scooted for safety. Minnows stopped feeding, and their actions became erratic. I had heard

Complete Angler's Library

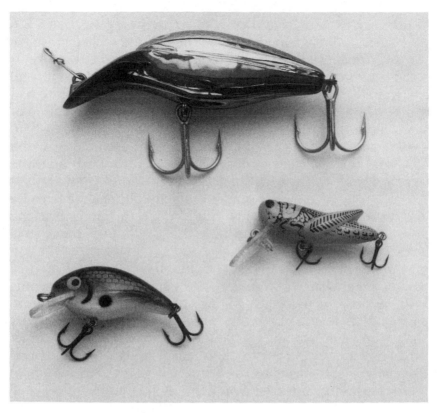

Lures such as the Rebel SST (top), the Crickhopper (right) and the Super Teeny-R (bottom) have a common feature. They create noise with internal rattles that generate strikes.

nothing but the peaceful sounds around me.

Then, a branch snapped upstream and a rock bounced noisily into the river. An angler pushed his way through the undergrowth. He dropped clumsily into the stream, and started casting. He fished lies where trout had been, but hooked nothing. Finally seeing me, he came over for a visit.

"Lousy fishing," he remarked, lighting a cigar. "You catch anything?"

"Not lately," I replied, hoping he wouldn't notice the long spine and ribs of the only one I hadn't put back. The bones had nearly burned in the embers of a small fire on the pebble beach.

After a bit of conversation the fisherman stood up and stretched.

"Guess I'll mosey down to the pool below, if you don't want

to fish it right now." He then nodded and was gone.

I quenched the dying embers of the fire and scuffed gravel to conceal it completely. Then, I took a short nap. As I awoke, a cloud bank from the west had moved in to obscure the sun. The big trout had resumed feeding and some smaller ones had reappeared. I slowly wriggled down the bluff to the protection of alder bushes and dropped a dry fly upstream of the rock where the big one lay. The fly fluttered down, drifted close to the rock, and the fish rose and took it. I backed the barb from the fish's jaw and watched it swim away.

Boat fishermen have a similar problem, although few realize it. The best way "not" to catch fish is to cut the motor over the hole . . . throw out the anchor . . . bang open the tackle boxes. You get the point.

Another mistake is to cast your lure too close to a fish. The plop of a crankbait, or even a spoon or spinner, can frighten it. Cast beyond the suspected hiding spot and fish the lure into position. Of course, there are exceptions to this. The quiet "splat" of a lure landing on the surface sometimes will attract fish. Frogs and even baitfish often make similar sounds. This is especially true at night, or in discolored water, because under these conditions, fish feed mainly by sound and scent.

Lures That Make Noise

Since fish feed by sound as well as by sight, several styles of lures are made to pop, splutter, chug, buzz, rattle, splash and vibrate. Even plastic worms give off sound audible to fish when inched and bounced along the bottom. The following are some typical ones:

Sonic lures are fish-shaped plugs with one or more attachment of eyes on the top of the body slightly forward of the dorsal fin position. By attaching the line to forward, middle or rear eyes, the lure can be fished at different depths with varying vibrations. These lures may have a vibrator-sound chamber to make them rattle or vibrate as the lure swims, but some emit only pulsating vibrations.

Spinners emit vibrations or pulsations to some degree. With their flashing, whirling blades, we think of them more as visual attractors. However, heavily-bladed ones also give off strong sound vibrations.

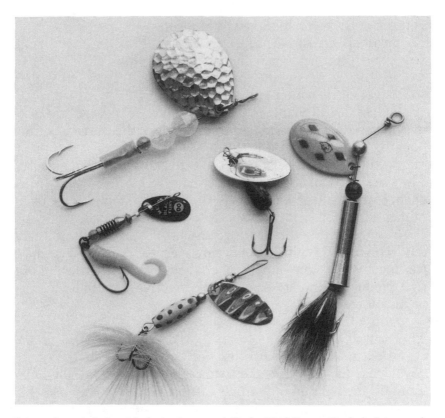

Spinner lures including (clockwise from top left) the Rigid Spoon, Dardevle Spinner, the Shyster and the Ultra-Lite Black Fury are in-line spinners that need to be fished rapidly for proper spinner action.

An instance of how sound attracts fish occurred on a canal off the Tamiami Trail on Florida's southern coast. The water was as discolored as it can get, a coffee-and-cream shade in which lures couldn't be seen inches under the surface. This was brackish water holding snook, but they ignored the streamer flies I was fishing so I switched to a large brass spinner and took fish on almost every cast. The other anglers immediately switched to pulsating lures and did the same. The place was loaded, but no fish were taken on lures that didn't emit sound. The point is that it was impossible for fish to see lures and they took them only by sound.

Spinners on lures splutter and splash on the surface, vibrate underneath, attracting fish by their sound. Underwater lures that wiggle also give off different sound vibrations. So do swimming baitfish which is why the lures work.

Splashers are surface lures which should be in every tackle box. The Jitterbug is a famous example. Its wide double lip pushes the water, while causing the bait to swim with a seductive wiggle which entices fish.

Poppers are available from tiny fly-rod size to large ones used in saltwater. When activated, they push the surface with a popping sound which adds to the visual effect.

Rattling lures are very effective regardless of water clarity. They are particularly useful in cloudy water and when fished deep. An excellent example is the Ratt-L-Trap. It has taken numerous big bass, in addition to pike and walleyes.

In summarizing the hearing sense of fish, three points stand out. The hearing of fish is amazingly acute. Anglers who make too much noise can ruin their chances of catching fish. Lures that produce sound are particularly effective, especially in deep or discolored water.

The Sense Of Smell

Science affirms the sense of smell in fish is highly developed, more so in some species than in others. The acute sense of smell of salmon, which can find their "home" rivers by following the faint, familiar scent they remember after years at sea is an example. The food morsels thrown into the water in chumming attract fish more by their scent than by the sight of the food itself. Sharks can zero in on the faint smell of blood in the water and find the source from far away.

Fish can detect and identify unseen members of their own species by their peculiar scent. Fish can also detect and find prey by scent. Some fish have repulsive odors, given them by heredity as a means of protection. You can rarely smell schools of fish in freshwater streams and lakes, either because you can't identify the odor or because the schools are too small to make it apparent. Expert saltwater anglers, however, often find big schools of fish by scent. A school of striped bass gives off an unmistakable odor of the herb called thyme. A school of bluefish can be found by the distinctive odor of cut melons wafting downwind.

In early spring, when streams are high and cold, experienced bait fishermen generally catch more trout than anglers who use artificial lures. The trout are resting in holding positions, and the bait must be presented to them so they can "smell" it even if they don't at first see it. To do this, cast upstream of the rock so the bait will sink and drift between the edges back of the rock. Casting *to* the rock won't work; the bait drifts above the fish and touches bottom, if at all, all too far downstream. The bait must be fresh to have maximum scent. A worm used a long time may look satisfactory, and may take fish by sight, but chances are much better with a fresh one which provides scent. If you are short of worms, puncture an old one with a hook so more scent can exude from it.

Scent has a bearing on taste. If a lure looks good, a fish may take it but will quickly expel it if it has an obnoxious taste. On many occasions, trout and salmon will go for a fly but won't take it. Fish may nip at flies without being hooked. This seems to be because of taste. Fish dislike human scent. Sometimes it seems that the fly or lure isn't taken until its obnoxious scent has washed off.

Old-time commercial fishermen have learned that it helps to dip lures in cod liver oil. One chap (who I'm sure is a good friend) sent me a small bottle of seal oil, supposedly to dip salmon flies in. A mere drop of this stuff in a salmon river will alarm fish far downstream because seals are enemies of salmon. At the same time, he sent me a small bottle of salmon oil, which may be useful. I'll take both bottles when I go fishing with him and ask him to dip his flies in them after I've hooked my limit!

Plastic worms are scented, usually with an extract of anise, which tastes like licorice. This is known to be an attractive scent to fish, although no one knows exactly why.

Fish in general, and particularly trout and salmon, find human scent repelling. For this reason, some anglers wash their hands on land before going fishing. Sosin and Clark state that while human scent is repulsive to fish, human saliva isn't. They say artificial flies will be taken more readily if the flies are moistened with saliva. This evidently substantiates the old maxim that, "You'll have better luck if you spit on your bait!"

3

How Water Temperatures Affect Fishing

Experienced fishermen agree that a thermometer or temperature probe is an important piece of fishing equipment. Fish are like people in seeking comfortable temperatures. Trout, bass and walleyes especially seek specific temperatures and cannot tolerate water of more than a few degrees variance. Members of the pike family (northern pike, muskellunge and pickerel), on the other hand, are contented in a much wider temperature range.

Science has provided definite information on the water temperatures preferred by various species of fish. When this was mentioned in Chapter 1, a temperature-activity table for freshwater fish was provided showing ideal temperatures preferred by the most important species and the surrounding range in which they can exist with reasonable comfort if they have to. This is restated in depth here for emphasis and clarification. Bluegills and sunfish prefer water of about 74 degrees, which is usually near the surface in summer, but they can be reasonably contented between 65 and 80 degrees. At the other end of the scale, lake trout prefer water of 41 degrees, but are more or less contented in a range between 40 and 50. This range is found in the depths of lakes in summer, so you have to fish deep. You will find lake trout on or near the surface after the ice melts in the spring or before freeze-up in the fall because their preferred temperature range is on or near the surface.

The trick is to fish at the ideal depth for whatever species

Finding the temperature zone in which the fish you are trying to catch is most comfortable is important no matter what time of day you fish. On a sunny morning in early spring, your quarry may be in shallow and warmer water.

How Water Temperatures Affect Fishing   37

you seek, knowing you may not hit it exactly but, if you're close to it, you should be reasonably successful.

What happens when fish can't find ideal temperatures, or a range in which they are reasonably comfortable? Take brook trout as an example. The ideal temperature for them is 58 degrees, and they should be active in streams of about that temperature, or at that temperature in ponds and lakes. They can get along in a range between 48 and 68 degrees, but are less and less inclined to take baits and lures as water temperature deviates from the ideal. So, suppose you're fishing when the trout season opens in the North and water temperature is near freezing, as it often is. Since this is below their tolerance range and they can't find water any warmer, the trout are less active and don't feed heavily. The only way to take them then is to present small lures or baits (preferably the latter) within mere inches of their mouths. However, their metabolism is so low that they may not take them even then. Under such icy-water conditions, I have seen big trout lying in the grass of high water near the surface close to shore, so cold they wouldn't move away unless prodded. They were in such shallow, exposed places because they were seeking the slight comfort of partially sun-warmed surface water there, but one could tickle their noses with a bait or lure without results.

Yet, opening days on a trout stream have such fascination for anglers that they get up long before dawn to be at their favorite spots by sunup. They may give up by midmorning because ice is collecting in the line guides, and they've had poor luck. The smart ones sleep late; arrive on streams nearer to noon, and are more successful because the sun (if there is any) has warmed the water a bit.

Conversely, when water is above 68 degrees and too warm for trout, they hug the bottom where it may be cooler, or they may seek the comfort of cold-water brooks or spring holes. Anglers who have taken stream temperatures know this, and avoid fishing warm-water areas. Trout that can't find cool water may die, because overly warm water is deficient in oxygen.

Water Temperature Effects Throughout The Year
Scientists have proved that fish can accurately seek their ideal temperatures to within a small fraction of a degree. This is

Favorite Water Temperature Depths of Principal Species
At Water Temperature Depth

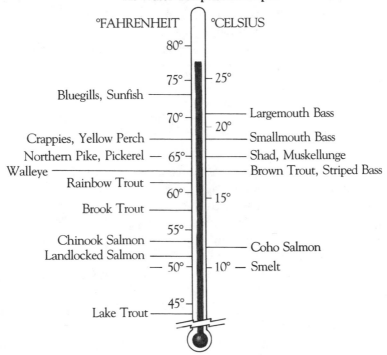

°FAHRENHEIT   °CELSIUS

- 80°
- 75° — 25°
  - Bluegills, Sunfish
- 70° — 20°   Largemouth Bass
  - Crappies, Yellow Perch ——— Smallmouth Bass
  - Northern Pike, Pickerel — 65° — Shad, Muskellunge
  - Walleye ——— Brown Trout, Striped Bass
  - Rainbow Trout
- 60° — 15°
  - Brook Trout
- 55°
  - Chinook Salmon ——— Coho Salmon
  - Landlocked Salmon
- — 50° — 10° — Smelt
- 45°
  - Lake Trout

These temperatures are close enough for good fishing, but may vary slightly between northern and southern regions due to acclimation. Tolerant temperatures vary a few degrees above and below the optimum ones given here. Members of the pike family acclimate themselves to a wide range of temperatures.

a relatively thin stratum in deep water. Getting lures down to it becomes complicated for two reasons. Even if we know the exact depth (which instruments can tell us), trolling at that precise depth entails the use of a downrigger, Dipsey Diver or unwieldy long line. In a later chapter, instruments that make it easier to troll at the proper depths will be discussed.

Secondly, there is a certain amount of flexibility to temperature tables because fish in different parts of the country become acclimated to slightly different temperatures. For example, a largemouth bass in the South, due to heredity, may be contented in water of nearly 80 degrees while one in the Midwest may be more comfortable to the charted 72-degree temperature.

Water thermometers for measuring surface temperatures are

inexpensive and widely available. All these tell you, however, is whether or not water near the surface approaches the ideal for the kind of fish you seek. If it does, near-surface fishing should be good in areas which satisfy other requirements of fish. If it doesn't, you'll have to work lures along the bottom in streams, fish deeper in lakes, or go to other waters where near-surface temperatures are more suitable.

When surface temperatures are too cold in rivers or streams, lures must be fished on or near the bottom. They should be small, and worked or drifted slowly. At such times, fish feed sparingly; they won't move far or much at all to take lures and usually take only small ones that require minimum exertion.

Water thermometers for measuring temperatures down deeper cost more because they are more complicated, but they are more useful. A typical one is shown here. It is about the size of a two-cell flashlight, with a dial at one end. A coil of wire wound around it is exposed by pulling both ends. The end of the wire is attached to a probe and a weight. Unwinding the wire lowers the probe and weight to the desired temperature depth which is recorded on the dial. This depth is marked in feet by reading the markings on the wire at water level.

Say, for example, that you are fishing a lake for rainbow trout. The temperature table tells you that the ideal temperature for rainbows is 61 degrees. The measured wire says this depth is 24 feet, so you know that is the depth to be fished. In general, you fish that depth where it touches bottom, the sides of the lake, or islands or reefs. Chapter 7 will explain this in greater detail.

How The Fall Turnover Affects Fishing

When taking temperature readings in lakes and deep ponds in the summer, you may be surprised to find that the temperature drops sharply at a certain depth. This level of rapid temperature change is called the "thermocline," and the best place to fish is right above it or in the upper portion of the change itself.

Water is heaviest (of greatest density) when it is at a temperature of 39.2 degrees Fahrenheit. Colder or warmer water is lighter and thus tends to rise to the surface and displace the heavier water which sinks. This causes drastic changes to

Spring Turnover

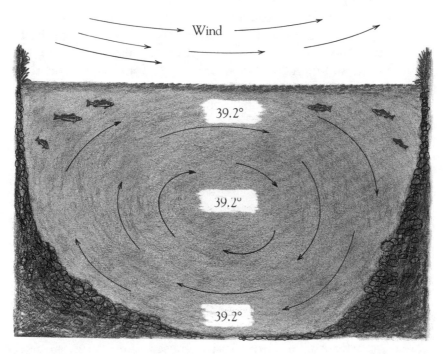

During spring turnover, the sun melts the ice and warms the water until it reaches maximum density of 39.2 degrees. Winds mix the water, equalizing the temperature; fish come to the surface to feed.

occur in lakes year-round. The illustrations show what happens during each season.

In winter, an insulating blanket of ice covers the lake in the northern states; the water below it is slightly above the freezing temperature of 32 degrees. Below this layer, the water becomes gradually warmer (and heavier) until the temperature of maximum density of 39.2 degrees is reached near the bottom. The presence of this relatively warmer water explains why lakes don't freeze solid in winter.

Aquatic plants provide food for baitfish, which in turn provide food for larger fish. But water plants need sunlight which helps them to absorb carbon dioxide and to give off oxygen in order to grow. There is a depth in deep lakes which sufficient sunlight does not penetrate. This depth depends on the clarity of the water and the amount of snow on the ice. Since at and below this depth there is insufficient plant life and oxygen, very few fish will be found there.

These facts provide tips on where to fish through the ice. We know that, in very cold water, fish seek the warmest temperatures they can find where there is also plant life to provide food and oxygen. These two conditions are met at the greatest depth where plant life exists, so you should cut your ice-fishing holes at positions above these areas. In shallow lakes, the deepest parts would be best, but structure, discussed in the next chapter, has a bearing on this. Since proper depth varies from lake to lake, you have to locate it by trial and error. A sounding can be taken of the depth of a productive hole, and other holes bored where the lake's contour is at this depth.

Hotspots for ice fishing are found where reefs rise from the lake bottom into a level of sufficient oxygen. They are found where underground springs pour relatively warm water into the lake, and where there are other bottom structure such as stream channels or sharp drop-offs.

As the spring sun warms the ice, it gradually melts and then suddenly disappears. This is the beginning of the "spring turnover period," which is of major importance to anglers. The increasing warmth of early spring raises the water surface temperature from near freezing to 39.2 degrees. At this time, all of the water in the lake is of approximately equal (and maximum) density. A wind blowing on the lake can therefore mix the surface water with the deeper water, actually causing all the water in the lake to churn, or "turn over."

When this equalizing of the temperature of the lake happens, fish that have been in the depths come to the surface and feed ravenously to make up for their period of semistarvation during the winter. In northern regions, fishermen wait for the call that "the ice is out," and hurriedly pack for a quick trip to their favorite lake. They may arrive a week or more too early! The fact that the ice has left doesn't mean that the lake has turned over, bringing hungry gamefish to the top. Winds turn the lakes over, and it may take a week or more after the ice goes out for this to happen. Find out when good fishing starts, and go there then.

In the case of wind blowing surface food to the eastern shore

Complete Angler's Library

Summer Stratification

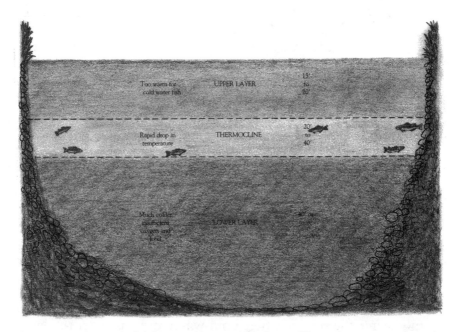

Too warm for cold water fish	UPPER LAYER	15' to 20'
Rapid drop in temperature	THERMOCLINE	20' to 40'
Much colder insufficient oxygen and food	LOWER LAYER	40' or more

Summer stratification finds lakes stratifying into three layers. The top layer is too warm and the bottom layer lacks sufficient oxygen. Fish inhabit the thermocline where temperature is constant all summer long.

of a lake, an angler would head to this shoreline which should be the most productive. But the surface water, if barely over 39.2 degrees, is still too cold for most species of fish. So they rest and feed in shallow areas where the sun has warmed the surface water.

On many early-season trips, big fish have been found lying as close as they can get to the shoreline, often in water too shallow for boats. The trick is to run the boat slowly within casting distance of the shoreline and to cast in as far as possible. Large fish may be lying in water almost too shallow to float these specimen.

The spring turnover stage and the fall turnover stage (wherein this process is reversed) are the two times during the year when cold-water fish such as lake trout and landlocked salmon can be caught near the lakes surface.

As spring progresses into summer, the surface water becomes increasingly warmer. Since it is warmer, and thus lighter than the water below, it stays on top. The warm layer generally meets the colder water at a depth of 20 feet or more, depending on the size of the lake and weather conditions. Where the warm layer meets the cold layer, a certain amount of mixing occurs, forming a third intermediate layer, the thermocline. This middle layer may be 20 feet or more thick, again depending on lake size and weather conditions. In any pond or lake, the temperature of the thermocline remains constant throughout the entire summer.

When choosing where they will spend the summer, cold-water fish shun the lower layer because it contains insufficient oxygen and food. They also shun the upper layer because it is too warm. Thus, they cruise in or very near the thermocline level where the temperature preference of each individual species suits it best.

In staying at this level, they also want to be near protection and food, which means that they usually will be found where this level meets the sides of the lake, or at this depth around islands and submerged reefs. They may leave the thermocline to come nearer the surface where cold-water streams enter the lake and, under certain conditions, they may come into the warm shallows in the evening or during the night to feed. During the summer, however, the thermocline level usually is the best bet.

The thermocline level can be found by taking readings at increasing depths with a temperature probe. For the first 20 feet or so, readings at 5-foot intervals will be very much the same. Then, suddenly, the instrument will indicate a rapid drop in temperature. The water will become rapidly colder as increasingly deeper readings are taken, and then the readings will level off when the probe goes below the thermocline. (The thermocline is the layer where the drop in temperature is at least one degree Centigrade per meter of depth.)

Thus, for the best summer fishing, you should stillfish or troll at the thermocline where it nears the lake bottom. If you can obtain a contour map of the lake (or want to bother to make one), you can chart the path of good trolling. You know the preferred water temperature of the fish you want to catch;

now, you are all set to translate this knowledge into action.

Shallow lakes or ponds may not stratify; long, narrow ones may stratify in the deep parts but not in the shallows. If no stratification is found, the answer is to fish the deeper parts because they are cooler and springs there may make certain areas comfortable for fish. Inlet streams provide cooler water, so their mouths may be hotspots in summer.

When fall arrives and cold nights lower surface water temperatures, the reverse of the spring turnover stage takes place. When surface water has cooled to 39.2 degrees, all the water in the pond or lake is of such similar density that wind action can mix it and equalize it at 39.2 degrees. Since the thermocline and the warm upper layer no longer exist, the fish which have been living at thermocline level, or near it, now come to the surface again and can be caught on top. Cold-water fish, such as lake trout, coho and landlocked salmon, provide top sport with surface lures around islands, reefs and shorelines. The fall turnover stage lasts until ice begins to form.

When the ice does begin to form, the winter stagnation period sets in and the annual cyclic behavior of northern lakes is completed.

Thus, if you want to fish for cold-water species, the best times to do it for greatest sport are during the weeks in the spring and in the fall when no thermal stratification exists and they can be caught on or near the surface. At such times, they are more lively than during summer or winter and provide better sport.

=4=

Shortcuts To Finding Fish

You've hired a guide, and are riding in the front seat of his boat. By reputation, he is a great angler. But it's been almost 45 minutes and you haven't dropped a line in the water.

Pretty expensive boat ride, you're beginning to think.

He's just driving along, staring at his depthfinder. Ten more minutes pass. Sharp turns, spins. The boat goes back against its own wake, rocking you until you grab the handrail, even though it's not windy.

"There they are," he finally says, one of those little guide's smiles cracking his lips open a quarter-inch for half a second. Satisfied about one thing, his head spins up to investigate.

You try to make conversation, but he can't hear you. He's looking for shore markings. He's glancing at the rods, to see if they're ready. They're ready. He looks down at the depthfinder every few seconds.

"Oh yeah," he says, "look at that."

It's time, finally, to start fishing.

You can't always catch fish even when you find them, but you certainly can't catch fish you can't find. Mike McClelland, arguably the most "quotable" professional angler of our time, likes to say, "The guy who puts the most baits past the most fish wins."

It's not a bad goal to shoot for. But before you can put any baits past any fish, you do have to track them down.

How do you find fish? It's one of the most talked-about subjects in modern fishing, but how much does the average angler really know about efficiently hunting for fish?

It seems that "the hunt" is something all professional anglers take for granted, but most "weekend" anglers tend to be spot fishermen. That is, they head out on the water, go straight to a "spot" and start to fish, ignoring the basic question "are there any fish here?"

They immediately start fishing, often with slow, methodical presentations (Hey, I wouldn't know so much about this if I wasn't as guilty as anybody.), usually spending too much time at each place. To compound the sin, they never look the spot over carefully, to see if fish might be deeper or shallower than they think. They have a few spots to check, and if the fish (a) aren't home, or (b) won't take the presentation they ram down their throats, the angler assumes "the fish aren't biting today." Usually, you find these anglers in town by noon, drinking beer at the Muni.

There are things you can do, regardless of your current ability, to become better at "hunting" for fish. And much of your success depends on what you do before you get into the boat, or walk down the shoreline to pick out a spot.

Assessing The Character Of A Body Of Water

Learn to assess the *character* of a body of water. In other words, before you look in microscopic detail at one or a few spots—before you choose where on that lake to start fishing—step back and study the entire picture.

You can gauge some things by looking at a contour map, but you have to be there to see other aspects. (This chapter won't go into detail on individual species. It will just point out the categories and what to look for. Still, it's up to you to know something about the fish you want to catch, and its seasonal tendencies. No matter what species you're after, it's probably not going to be in the same types of spots in summer as winter, for example. And, a location that holds smallmouth bass might not hold largemouth bass; one loaded with crappies might not have many walleyes or northern pike. Where you concentrate your efforts hinges, in a lot of cases, on what you're after.)

Get a "quick read" of potential high-percentage areas by

looking at the following things:

First, study the overall basin of the body of water. What options does it offer the fish? Even if you read in books that "bass like to patrol weedlines," what if the lake has bass but no weedlines? The fish can't hop a train to a lake with classic weedlines. Realize that fish have to live in the environment they're given.

What Kind Of Fishery Is It?

Is it a shallow, dishpan lake? It might have only one deep hole, which would be an important fish location at times. If it has three such holes, you're going to want to check them all. In the absence of any obvious deep holes or other classic breaks, the fish might relate more to weeds (when present), any brush or other cover, any subtle changes in depth, and changes in bottom composition. A lake like this often doesn't have many "fish magnets" as pros call them—locations that tightly bunch fish. Therefore, you might be dealing with a lot of scattered fish that are best pursued with a fast-moving style such as trolling crankbaits.

Or, is it a moderately deep lake with a few classic structures? In some ways, these are the "easiest" lakes to figure out quickly. There might be two obvious points, for example, one of which leads into the only deep-water basin in the entire lake. The drawback to a spot like this, unless it's in Alaska, is that everybody and his mother-in-law pounds it to death on a day-to-day basis.

Or, is it a heavily structured basin with numerous deep-water zones? This kind of lake can be intimidating, to say the least. Where to begin? It's not as hopeless as it seems.

Look at the layout of the structural elements. Some, even though they look good on the map, will be isolated, off by themselves. Other areas will be more "complex and varied;" that is, groups of structural elements will be in proximity to one another. These areas offer a better balance of deep- and shallow-water zones, and are usually more consistent fish producers. Again, though, this is a general statement; some fish species, at some seasons, might have a tendency to suspend in open water. Structure, by itself, is no guarantee of success.

Shallow feeding zones—often called "food shelves"—near

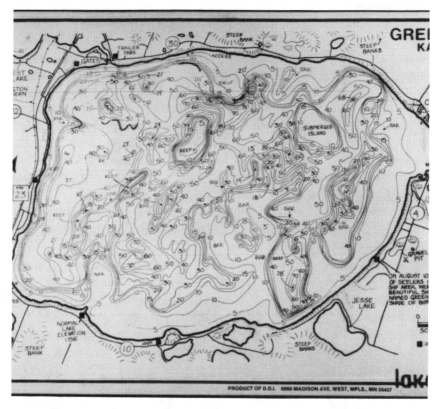

Too much of a good thing? Some lakes have lots of structural elements. These are arguably the hardest bodies of water to quickly locate fish on. One great shortcut is to locate groups of structural elements; that is, "complex" areas, as opposed to structures that are isolated.

deep water are one of the constants, however, when it comes to fish location. Not for all species, but for many. The best food shelves are also complex in makeup, having irregular "stair-step" ledges, a variety of bottom types and cover.

Analyzing Water Clarity

Also, look at the water clarity. Some lake maps have information on clarity and the reasons for any staining. This is useful information, but clarity can vary widely from day to day, due to wind, time of year (turnover, for example, stirs up sediments and clouds even clear-water lakes), and other variables. It's best to judge clarity with your own eyes, on the day you're going to fish.

Water clarity can be an important clue to fish location.

Many species won't spend a lot of time in shallow, clear water in bright-light conditions, for example. Or, if they do, it's usually in the shadowed zones in and around weeds and other cover. You might (again, depending on species) expect to find more fish in deep water, if the water is clear.

Dirtier water, on the other hand, can shelter big fish at extremely shallow depths. Dirty water often doesn't make for good weed growth, and weeds don't usually grow except in the shallows. You have to be careful of this, because some "dirty" water is simply stained, which can allow surprisingly deep sunlight penetration, and weed growth. It's difficult to make generalizations about fishing, but keep in mind that dirtier water often means shallower gamefish—and clearer water often means deeper gamefish.

Water clarity can also be a clue as to when a fishery might be at its best. Clear-water lakes can often yield their best catches under low-light conditions, when fish move more freely and feed more aggressively. "Low light conditions" means heavy overcast days, stormy weather, dusk and dawn, after dark, and anytime heavy waves wrinkle the surface and cut light penetration.

Dirty-water lakes are often the opposite, yielding their best catches when light penetration gets highest, giving predators a better look at prey. These guidelines, while not flawless, can be a useful starting point.

Finding Open-Water "Basin" Fish

After top anglers taught many fishermen to find and fish structural elements, fish and structure became glued together in their minds. Find structure and you find fish. Fish are always "relating" to structure in some way.

The reality, anglers have come to learn, is that fish often hold on or near structure, assuming environmental conditions (water temperature, oxygen levels and light levels) are favorable and food is found on the structure. "But," says Mike McClelland, "a fish doesn't say to himself, 'Boy, look at that nice rock pile; I think I'll go over there for a while.' He doesn't sit on a nice rock pile and starve to death. He won't be there unless his food is there."

Anglers have come to learn that much fish food is found in

the middle of nowhere at certain times of year. They've learned, through the efforts of tournament anglers like Keith Kavajecz and Gary Parsons, that a lot of fish—and big ones, too—can be caught by plying the open basin waters, sometimes miles from any structure.

These fish are sometimes called "suspended," but they can be on or near bottom. And anglers now think of them as completely disassociated from structure, but some of them are "structure" fish that have slid off, horizontally, from structure—either after feeding, to chase moving baitfish, or as a reaction to fishing or boating pressure.

But how in the world do you efficiently search for open-water fish, especially in places like the Great Lakes?

Parsons and Kavajecz have a system. Here are the highlights which will make you a better basin troller:

● Rumors about certain general areas that kick out a lot of fish can get you started in the right direction.

● Always have your sonar unit running, and keep your boat speed at a level that allows a readable display, as you move from spot to spot. Be looking for fish and baitfish as you cross basins. (A large bay can be a basin.)

● If you see fish, set lines to troll. Crankbaits are a good choice. Don't even blink while you purchase a copy of Mike McClelland's book *Crankbaits*, and one of his *Crankbait Trolling Depth Guides*. They are the only sources of their kind. They tell you how deep more than 200 lures run, on different line weights, and with differing lengths of line out. You can set lines to a variety of depths, after choosing from a variety of lures with differing actions and wobbles. You don't know, ahead of time, what action will trigger strikes.

One important note: Always set at least one line to run shallow, about 3 to 6 feet. Even if you don't see any shallow fish on the depthfinder, they can be there. It's a deadly sin to ignore this possibility!

Now make trolling passes, the scope of which are determined by the size of the area to be covered. Parsons and Kavajecz normally track their passes on the plotter function of a Loran-C unit. Then, as they make each successive pass, it's easy to run a parallel path.

These pros don't cover the same area twice, until they

contact fish. When they catch fish, they record the location as a waypoint in their loran. In this methodical manner, they can actually chart the size and location of an open-water school of fish, which can be huge! They can stay with schools as they move on successive days, by first returning to the fish's previous location, then branching out in each direction until contacting them again—always keeping track of boat movements on the loran.

● Even if you don't have a Loran-C unit, or fish in an area where loran reception isn't good, you can try to be precise. If the area isn't too big, take shore markings and compass headings as you make each trolling pass. It'll help you avoid covering the same area more than once. When you catch fish, take shore markings again and write them down for your future reference.

Analyzing A Specific Lake
Also, take a hard, objective view of the specific body of water you're on. Again, ask yourself the question: What options does this lake offer the fish?

A lot has been said about weeds. In some regions (Arizona reservoirs being a prime example), there are virtually no weeds. There, fish-collecting structure consist mainly of various sized rocks, with some scattered scrub brush in shallow coves.

Many of the breaks into deep water are more like vertical bluffs you could skydive from, if they were above water. Fish hold on minute crevices along these steep bluffs, and along transition zones between bottom types. The point, again, is that everything is relative. Fish make do with the environment they are born or planted in; they don't know that their cousins three states away are lounging in lush cabbage weeds, and they don't care. They are busy making a living in the water they are stuck with.

If your lake is filled with flooded timber, look for the thickest stands of the biggest trees and you'll probably find fish. But don't expect to find a fish behind every stump.

If your lake is thick with weeds, it's going to be difficult to present a lure. Look for pockets in the weeds, and work lanes and edges. If there's only one decent-sized weedbed, approach it quietly and spend a lot of time working it. It probably holds

Structure isn't always the answer! Many fish can be caught—especially in midsummer—by systematically trolling the open waters of a lake's "basin" zones.

some of the biggest fish in the lake.

And don't ever forget the possibility that a lot of fish—catchable fish, especially during the summer months—might be patrolling open water, away from structure.

Also, consider weather conditions while planning strategy. Has the weather been stable, warming, or has a monster cold front arrived? That will change what you should do.

In general, stable weather makes for more aggressive fish, and their "strike zones" (the distance they're willing to move to hit a bait) are relatively large. A cold front usually puts fish off their feed. They might drop into deep water or tuck up tight to cover, where they become hard to catch. You might have to tease bites with slow presentations.

Whatever the situation on the lakes you fish—or if you find yourself vacationing on a lake type you've never encountered—going through this mental review should lead you to likely fish locations, and methods for catching them.

Keys To Quickly Finding Fish
• Don't do a lot of fishing—unless maybe you troll while

looking things over—until you see fish, or at least baitfish or other food sources. In deeper water, you'll have to rely on sonar; in shallower water, you can sometimes see fish, minnows being chased, freshwater shrimp, frogs or other things.

• Don't spend a lot of time looking over, or fishing, a lot of the same type of territory. If you cast a lure around the rim of three lily-pad-filled bays and catch one small fish, don't go to a fourth lily-pad-filled bay. Look deeper, or in different kinds of weeds. Or in the open water of a deep basin. Systematically scope out different locations until you find a pattern.

• Even when you do find a successful pattern, don't assume it's the only one! Results of competitive bass and walleye tournaments have proven that a variety of fish-catching patterns can be "going" at once, on the same body of water.

• Until you locate fish and establish a pattern, fish quickly. In most cases, that means choosing a "horizontal" presentation that can be moved along: a live-bait rig or spinner behind a heavy bottom bouncer, a crankbait, or maybe casting a spinnerbait through high-percentage water.

If you believe a slow presentation is the only way to tempt bites, don't spend all day trying it on the same spot. In that case, fish quickly by limiting the amount of time you spend at each stop.

• And now, the main rule of all:

If things that should work don't, toss out all the rules and start looking where the fish shouldn't be, and start trying presentations they shouldn't be interested in. The open-minded approach has won a lot of money for tournament anglers, and it can save many a slow day for you.

Complete Angler's Library

Reading
Water

5

Using Electronics
Efficiently

Many anglers—even those who go fishing a lot—can find it intimidating, not to mention humbling, to watch a great angler use electronic aids to catch fish.

After all, you get amazed enough watching a truly top-notch small stream angler, somebody like Gary Borger, quickly read water flows and make flawless casts to high-percentage spots. Trout you only dream about commit themselves to his flies more often than anyone would believe.

Yet, learning to recognize something you can see with your eyes, like visible stream currents, is a tangible skill to strive for. It takes years of practice, along with a teaspoon of natural talent, but most anglers who put their mind to it have confidence they can become half-good at it.

But human beings can't see through water—at least not more than a few feet of calm, clear water on a sunny day. So when we watch somebody who's good at using sonar to hunt up high-percentage fishing spots, to pick out fish near the bottom, to decide whether they're catchable, it stirs up strong feelings of inadequacy, of desperation.

How're you gonna get good at that?

I'll never forget the first time I hopped in the boat with legendary pro fisherman Gary Roach. Many of you know who he is, a man known as "Mr. Walleye" even to fellow pros. His silver beard and knowing eyes say it all: He's been across the

A master angler like Gary Roach can make sonar use look like magic. But, by learning how sonar works, and putting in some practice time (perhaps with an experienced angler) you, too, can learn to see underwater structure, cover and fish.

lake and back a few times.

This was a number of years ago, but it's still fresh in my memory. All I wanted to do was watch him, watch everything he did. His flasher ran exactly the way mine did, but he was picking up all this information that I never saw on mine.

"There, see that?" he'd say. "We just passed off that hard spot, and we're back onto the mud. Let's see if there's any suspended fish out here . . .

"Nobody home . . . let's slide back up onto the hump. Oooh, there's a bunch of bait . . . oooh, see that? That was a walleye. Oooh, see that?"

I shook my head "yes" for him, another way to myself.

But after a few hours of sitting on his cooler, just off his right shoulder, it started becoming easier to identify fish.

Using Electronics Efficiently

It seems like a long time since sonar came into general use on small fishing boats, but it hasn't been a generation.

Maybe the troubles most anglers have with learning to use sonar stem from the fact that until about 10 or 15 years ago, they were still using manual typewriters. Telephones had plastic wheels with holes in them, and you stuck your finger in the number you wanted to dial. It took some reasoning power to write a letter or decide who to call, but a monkey could operate the equipment.

What does that have to do with sonar, and fishing? Some think this generation of anglers didn't have the benefit of watching their parents, or other mentors, use sonar. "Fishfinders" were something magical that came out not too long ago, after a lot of anglers already learned something about fishing, and they were complicated to use. They tried, but a lot of them are still using them to make the boat look modern in the driveway.

Too many anglers are sonar-illiterate; they might be able to tell how deep the water is, and they might not. What they think they see is probably not what's down there, but they need to sound positive about it, like their heroes do on television.

A skill needs to be developed, one that most anglers lack. You have to be able to look at a displayed echo—whether it's a flasher blip, or a marking on a paper graph or liquid crystal display—and see something other than a mysterious echo. Your mind has to be trained to see fish, in all their detail. It also needs to be trained to see different structure, such as weeds, tree stumps and hard or soft bottoms.

Not a blip, not a scratch, but a fish!

Today, kids try in vain to teach their parents and grand-parents how to program a video cassette recorder. The next generation of anglers, it seems, will be more comfortable with electronic devices, well-equipped to take sonar on the water and make the mental transformation it requires to realize that a blip on the screen is information—perhaps a fish or a weed —and not just a blip on the screen.

Understanding Sonar

Before you can improve your ability with sonar, you have to know something about how it works.

Complete Angler's Library

Your sonar unit, whether flasher, paper graph, liquid crystal or video, sends an electrical signal down the power cord to the transducer. (The transducer is that blob of plastic shaped like a hockey puck, or maybe a spear point, that makes a direct connection with the water.)

The transducer converts the electrical impulse into sound waves, which can travel through water. The sound waves power their way down until they bump into the bottom or other things that reflect them, such as fish, baitfish, weeds, downrigger balls or algae. (An "echo" can be made by anything of different density than water, harder or softer. According to sonar experts, for example, a steel ball bearing and an air bubble—one much denser than water, the other much less dense—could produce similar echoes.)

The reflected sound waves from these objects, in the form of echoes, bounce back to the transducer, where they are received and again changed into electrical impulses. Those impulses—based on how long they took to go down and come back—are displayed on the screen or dial at different "depths."

Believe it or not, one signal is sent down, returns and is displayed before another is released! This sounding rate varies from brand to brand. Also, it's faster when units are set to shallower depth ranges; slower when being used in deeper water. It happens incredibly fast. A rate of 10 times per second is commonly reached by many units.

The area of coverage of the sound waves, usually called the cone angle, is roughly the shape of an inverted water balloon. The strongest signals—those likely to pick up smaller or weaker "targets" like baitfish and weeds—are those traveling straight or almost straight down. As you move away from center, the signals get weaker. That's why you'll hear people say that it's difficult to pick up fish at the "edge of the cone."

(All modes of sonar—flashers, paper graphs, liquid crystals, videos and digital readouts—work exactly this same way. The major difference among them is in how they display the information they gather.)

Now, there is a critical thing to understand:

How high you turn up the sensitivity, or gain, will have a dramatic affect on how much information the unit provides.

Even though it's not a perfect analogy, compare the

sensitivity control of a sonar unit to the "brightness" control of your television. By turning the brightness level all the way up, the television picture turns completely black and becomes meaningless, even though the set is turned on. The set is picking up the broadcast, but you can't see it well.

You can adjust the brightness until you "sort of" see the program, but you have to work hard at it. You have to know ahead of time what you're looking for, and you have to know the handicap you're up against. By experience, people know how to adjust the brightness to get a comfortable picture, so everything they want to see is clearly visible.

It's not much different with sonar!

Now picture this: Your boat is in 24 feet of water, over a rock hump. Two big fish are almost directly under you, and numerous baitfish 5 feet above them. You come putt-putting along with your outboard, trying to look the spot over with your sonar to examine its contents.

But, you've just barely turned the sensitivity control up high enough to have the unit running. You're getting a faint signal at 24 feet, and you have a feeling that its the bottom. Do you think those big fish or the baitfish are showing up? No way. Signals are hitting them, of course. Full force, in fact, with as much power as the unit is capable of generating.

(The sensitivity control governs how much the returning echoes are amplified, but the transmitting power of the unit is normally fixed. That is, if you have a 600-watt unit, it puts out 600 watts in 2 or 200 feet of water. The same amount of echo power is being received at the transducer regardless of the sensitivity setting. But weaker echoes don't get displayed at low sensitivity settings.)

So, all the fish echoes in this example are being received by the transducer and sent to the unit. But, if sensitivity is set so low that the bottom is barely being displayed, the receiver hasn't been made "sensitive" enough to pass the weaker fish echoes on to the display.

What else is wrong? The bottom signal is faint! You're over solid rock! If the sensitivity were turned up to where it should be, a thick, bright bottom signal would be glaring back on a flasher, or a wide bottom signal that perhaps has a thick "grayline" zone under it on a paper graph, liquid crystal or

Adjusting Sensitivity For Best Readings

The amount of detail a sonar unit displays depends strongly on how high the sensitivity control is set. The unit picks up all the detail regardless of sensitivity setting, but you have to amplify the signal by adjusting sensitivity, or it won't show up on the display. Too much is as bad as too little as the signal can become "too full of information" and be confusing.

video. And if you're using a flasher, a definite "second echo," at twice the bottom depth, would appear as well.

Is it making sense? What you see on a sonar unit depends heavily on how high or low you set the sensitivity. (There are other factors, such as whether you're getting electrical interference from other devices in your boat, or interference from other nearby boats that are also operating sonar units at a similar frequency as yours. If you don't know how to install sonar, pay a professional to do it for you. According to sonar manufacturer estimates, at least 80 percent of operating problems reported by anglers, who are otherwise good at using their units, are due to improperly installed transducers.)

Always experiment with the sensitivity setting, until you become comfortable with your unit. You want that thing set to the "edge" of where it starts to fill the screen with too much information. Sensitivity can be safely set higher when you slow the boat down for a close look at things (you want to see as many details as possible, and slower speeds create fewer interference problems, letting you increase sensitivity). Also, you can bump it up as you get into deeper water and over softer bottoms.

There is a point, though, if you keep turning it up, where the unit becomes too sensitive and the display fills with information. (Sort of like the television set when the brightness is too high; the whole display goes "black.")

Just remember that the general idea, no matter what type of sonar you have, is to turn up that sensitivity, so the unit can show you all the little details, like cover, baitfish and gamefish.

Many of today's liquid crystal and video units have automatic modes, where sensitivity is adjusted for you. How well do these modes work? Some work better than others, as you might expect.

Older models usually have the sensitivity pre-set too low to do a good job of showing you important details when you need them most—after slowing down for serious fishing. That leaves you handicapped when it comes to seeing smaller targets like fish and baitfish, according to Allan Tarvid, a Texas-based outdoor writer and sonar authority.

He says factory engineers building today's less sophisticated units have to settle for "an average level that should be best for most people in a variety of circumstances," accounting for potential high-speed running problems such as (a) mechanical noise, or acoustic interference from the engine and boat hull; and (b) electrical interference from trim motors, pumps, and the engine's charging and ignition systems.

Check whether your unit allows you to "bias" the automatic sensitivity setting up or down, while leaving the unit in automatic mode. If it does, it should do a good job, when adjusted, as described, to changing conditions.

State-of-the-art automatic modes are getting better all the time. Eagle and Lowrance, for example, have "Advanced Signal Processing" that is like a "smart automatic." It constantly increases or decreases sensitivity, and even adjusts various suppression features, to account for faster and slower boat speeds, changing bottom densities, and a variety of other interference levels.

"It manages the unit's features about as well as almost any person could," says Tarvid, not normally one to trust automatic sonar. "Ninety percent of the people probably couldn't run the system better than the machine does it."

(One warning: Liquid crystals that can be programmed to display fish as little "fishies," called "Fish ID" or something similar, are not highly prized by experts. For one thing, filters in the programs normally cut out surface clutter, which can be a valuable clue to water clarity. Also, they tend to show anything similar in density to a bigger fish—from a tightly-grouped bunch of baitfish, to sticks, to insignificant stuff like water bubbles and even algae concentrations—as a bigger fish.)

As a rule, it's not a good idea to rely too heavily on fish ID images, no matter how cute the fishies.

A Quick Word About Suppression

Virtually all modern sonar units have adjustable suppression controls of various kinds. They help the unit keep interference (electrical or air bubbles) from being displayed. But suppression also lessens the unit's ability to distinguish between objects that are close together, such as fish that are close to the bottom, or near each other.

With suppression turned up, a group of baitfish can look like a monster bass or walleye. You don't want that, so don't turn up suppression unless you absolutely have to. About the only time you might need it—assuming your unit is properly installed—is when you're running across a lake at high speed. But I've seen well-rigged units that worked at extremely high speeds with no suppression. That's what you should strive for.

How Do You Get Good?

You become good at using sonar by practicing with it. As simple as that sounds, nobody does it.

The day you buy a personal computer for your home, do you sit down and write a novel on it? Or lay out all your tax records on Lotus? Yet, people want to buy a sonar unit, slap it on their boat, and "get in the game."

You motor out in the middle of nowhere, turn the thing on,

and try to interpret all the confusion in front of your buddies. Of course, you don't admit you're just starting to use it. Of course, you didn't read the owner's manual.

Even if you've been using sonar for years, it's a safe bet you've never practiced your skills with it. Try a few simple things:

• Go to a lake with clear water. Starting at shore, turn on your sonar unit and drive away into somewhat deep water, but never deeper than you can see bottom (if you can get into 10 feet, that's great). Travel from soft to hard bottom to see what the bottom signal does. If you have a liquid crystal that adjusts sensitivity automatically, see if it does a good job.

Go over boulders, and matted weeds, and through thick weeds. Teach yourself to interpret the signals. If you do this for an hour or so, even flashers—famous for being "hard to understand"—make sense.

• Now, venture out deeper. You may have to turn the sensitivity up a bit to keep all the information coming in "loud and clear." Motor out until the bottom drops off relatively quickly. That's called a shoreline break, something you may have never found in your life!

Turn, and try to follow the shoreline break all the way around the lake, or the bay if it's a big lake. You'll see that the breakline is straight in some places, and gets uneven in others. Major shoreline-connected points become easy to see; you'll have to turn out into the lake to stay with the break. These are good fishing spots, for many species, at various times of the day and year.

(Most major shoreline points are easy to find on lake maps, which will be talked about in the next chapter. But also be on the lookout for smaller, less obvious points, and their accompanying inside turns, which are the opposite of a point. Out-of-the-way spots are often better than well-known "community spots" that everybody fishes.)

• Now, being careful, start at one shoreline and cut straight across the lake. Have the sensitivity set high enough so that even when you get into deeper water, the unit can pick up lots of small details, even baitfish. If you can't get a good "high-speed reading," take your boat to a good service center and ask them to check your transducer installation. Often, the

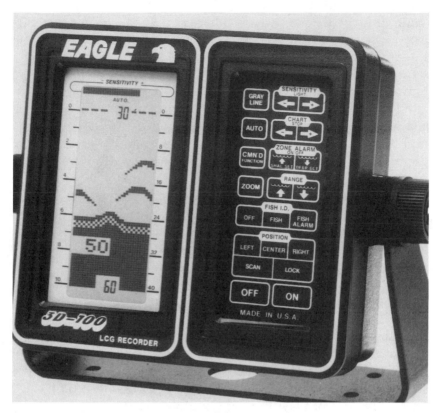

Liquid crystal units such as this one provide a lot of information once an angler becomes familiar with its use. This one works off of a scanning-style transducer.

transducer isn't mounted in a good spot, or positioned at the proper angle.

Pay attention to how the bottom composition gets harder and softer. Look for suspended fish, out "in the middle of nowhere." When you least expect it, in fact, you might find a small hard-bottomed hump. It might not even be on the lake map! If you do find something, take shore sightings or punch the "Waypoint Save" button on your Loran-C unit.

Don't expect to become a sonar whiz in one weekend, or even a whole season. Start slowly, like this, making sure you understand "what that thing tells you" as Gary Roach likes to say. Most people forget how to learn as they get older, because they get too impatient and skip through the learning phase.

Within a year or two, though, it'll become second nature.

Your mind will "see" weeds when a display characteristic of weeds appears on the screen; a hard bottom when the bottom signal widens; and, when others around you might see only a scratch on the sonar screen, the flaring gills of a big fish will jump out, loud and clear.

Then, the next step is to start seeing the big picture. You should be able to run zig-zags across an entire lake, or big bay, and come away with a picture in your mind of the bottom contours. Don't look only at the current display. Try to remember where you've been, and think about where you're headed. Play "connect the displays" in your mind.

Does the lake have fast-breaking shores or slower tapers? Where are the massive areas of deep water? Are there any hard-bottom areas tucked away, that most anglers possibly don't know about?

After you can see clearly through your underwater eyes, you'll know in a matter of minutes.

Flashers Vs. "Graphs"

Tradition teaches that you should use a flasher for high-speed running, to look over the lake. Then, when you slow down to "really fish," shut the flasher off and turn on some type of picture-display unit, or graph.

That's still pretty good advice, because a well-installed, modern-day flasher is the king of high-speed performance. No matter what anyone tells you, the display on a flasher "updates" (shows you fresh information) faster, and more often, than other sonar types.

When people say that a flasher just doesn't show them the details that their graph does, they're actually saying they have a harder time understanding the flasher reading, which is true in many cases. If you haven't spent much time with a flasher, it is harder to read than the two-dimensional picture on a liquid crystal, video or paper graph.

But all the detail is there on a flasher. In fact, it's the least "processed" information you'll ever receive from a sonar unit. (Something has to "translate" the signals coming into a graph-type display, or you won't see the scratches and "hooks" of fish, for example.) Probably, that explains why the flasher can update its signal so fast over changing structure.

Working A Shoreline Break

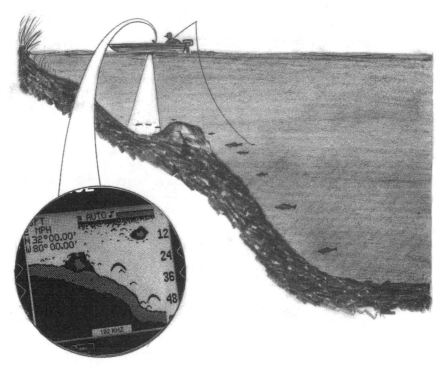

This illustration indicates what the angler is seeing on the LCG screen as he works a shoreline break. The "newest" information will start showing up at the left-hand side of the screen.

One drawback to flashers is their lack of "history" on the dial. You have to be staring at a flasher dial, at all times, or you might miss something. However, you can just glance occasionally at a graph display and catch up on the past few seconds.

More and more serious pros are relying on their liquid crystals and video units, for searching bottom contours, looking for fish and zeroing in for the catch. Properly installed, for example, liquid crystals work fairly well at moderate speeds, making them better than they used to be for "search mode."

You should probably get the sonar unit that you're most comfortable with. A flasher is still hard to beat for a lot of things, even if it is arguably more difficult to master. For several reasons, not the fact that they are far-and-away the finest ice-fishing sonar (which we'll get to in Chapter 10), you hear fewer rumors about flashers dying away completely.

If there's one piece of sonar advice that all anglers should hear, it's read the owner's manual. The manual gets tossed aside by new owners in a hurry to be on the water. They contain priceless insight into using the particular unit you purchased.

Other than that, the biggest shortcut to sonar proficiency is a day in the boat with a veteran angler, someone who has taken the time to learn what sonar can do. Get over their shoulder, start with the most basic questions you have, and forget about putting a line in the water that day.

Because every outing after that, you'll be paid back, with interest.

"Other" Electronic Aids

A number of other electronic gadgets can help you become a better angler. But, most space has been devoted to mastering sonar because it is the most important skill needed for finding fish and understanding the underwater environment.

Here are some quick points about these gadgets. That does not mean that, in some cases, they are not important.

● Loran-C: Many of you are familiar with loran units, which have become more affordable every year. As long as you are fishing somewhere within reach of the transmissions from the chains of radio towers necessary for that loran operation, you can return to those hotspots you've found with the help of steering instructions from the unit!

To a degree, you can get loran coordinates from other anglers, or off loran-marked maps. But finding a spot with your unit, from coordinates originally discovered with another unit, does not always work out well. Keep that in mind.

Loran can be a wonderful safety device, especially for big-water boaters. But be aware that extremely heavy rain, and thunder and lightning between your boat and a loran tower can cause that tower's signal to be lost. The farther you are from the tower, the worse the problem. However, thanks to far-sighted professional fishermen like Keith Kavajecz and Gary Parsons, loran is also becoming a powerful fishing tool.

● Temperature gauges: Water temperature can be important to fish location, especially at certain times such as spawning, turnover and summer when warm surface temperatures can drive some fish deep.

Many sophisticated liquid crystal and video sonar units come with surface temperature gauges. They are also available as options from several manufacturers. Either way, a probe has to be mounted to the outside of your boat.

Temperature depth probes with which you can check the water temperature at different depths are also available. They make it easy to check for thermoclines in summer, for example, where lighter surface water stacks on top of denser, cooler water. As discussed in a previous chapter, many fish will sit on, slightly above, or in the thermocline, making it important to fish location. Some lakes exhibit multiple thermoclines. Wind can stack up warmer water at one end of a lake, doing away with thermoclines, or raising or lowering their depth from one place to another.

(Thermoclines can often be spotted on sonar units, including flashers, if the units are adjusted properly. Usually, you have to turn up the sensitivity as high as you can, while still leaving a readable display. All suppression [noise-rejection] features must be turned off, including any "Fish I.D." feature.)

Some fish, like open-water lake trout, can be very temperature sensitive during certain seasons, so finding exactly the right band of water is important in catching them.

Hand-held units require you to lower the probe manually. Probes can also be attached to a downrigger ball, making deep-water temperature checks easier. Shop for equipment that fits your budget and style of fishing.

Trolling speed indicators: No mystery about what these do. In some cases, lure speed is the variable that triggers strikes—and it can change from day to day, even hour to hour. Why can't you just return the boat's throttle to the same setting and assume you're going the same speed you were on the last pass? Because moving with, against—or sideways to—wind or current can make it difficult to repeat trolling speed with complete accuracy.

Again, many liquid crystal and video sonar units come with trolling speed indicators.

Marine radios: Thought of as primarily a piece of safety equipment—they are wonderful for that purpose alone—

For a top pro angler like Roach, a nice catch like this is the reward for learning how to use electronics effectively for fishing.

marine-band radios are also used to keep in touch with fellow anglers on the water. Let's say you and your friends, using three boats, want to fish a new lake. You all have radios, and split up to fish different areas. When someone finds fish, he or she can let the others know right away, without having to run all over looking for them.

Spotlights: You know, those 15-million-candlepower jobs that double as bug zappers. You may have to check with game wardens for local rules about this, but many veteran anglers use them to "spot" fish at night in shallow water.

Spending some time on the water at night can reveal at least general areas that fish are using—sort of akin to looking for animal tracks in the mud! In some cases, the fish will even be in those shallow-water locations during the day.

Top pro angler McClelland believes people don't catch shallow-water fish at midday because they spook them before they can present a lure to them. If you see big fish in a shallow area at night, try making long casts, or perhaps trolling lures into the area using planer boards, keeping your boat as far away as possible, during daytime fishing.

Who knows what might happen.

Color selectors: Some great anglers have this to say about color selectors. There is serious doubt whether the instruments available to the angler work very well, for one thing. For another, it's a matter of priorities.

The main thing is to find fish, and present a lure or bait to them, making it easy for them to eat it if they want to. Anglers probably spend way too much time, says McClelland, worrying about whether they have the right color lure on, and not enough worrying about the more important variables.

It may come down to fish being selective about color from time to time. It may be important to know what color the fish can see best in a given water clarity and depth. But, as a general rule, use tried-and-true colors that certain species have fallen for in the past.

It's impossible to go into detail for every species. But if you're confused, try this simple formula. Start with fluorescent colors in dirtier water, and more subtle, natural (silver, gold) colors in clearer water. Try phosphorescent (glow-in-the-dark) in very dirty water, deep water, at night and perhaps during extreme low-light conditions such as heavy rainstorms.

But, if you're not catching fish—and you are satisfied you're paying most of your attention to more important details like fish location—experiment. Rules are broken every day by the fish.

6

Using Maps

Very rare, indeed, is the angler who doesn't follow the crowd. Striking off on your own, even on a small lake, is intimidating unless you believe in your ability to find fish.

At practically every lake you fish, there is probably a group of boats working a potentially good spot. But somebody, at some time, had to find that spot without much help.

Chances are, a lake map provided most of the clues.

A map could probably also help any of those boats find a similar spot that they could have all to themselves. A spot they would whisper about later at supper. A spot where the fish are not being pressured, where they bite more readily.

It's a good thing sonar use was discussed before diving into map use. Except when fishing from shore (and lake maps help a lot for that, which will be discussed), you'll need sonar skills to get the most from lake maps.

What are lake maps? (The word "lake" is being used generically here, to mean lakes, rivers, reservoirs and ponds.) You'll hear them described as "topographic" maps, "hydrographic" maps, "contour" maps, "topo" maps, "bottom" maps, "structure" maps, and who knows what else. Like a sonar display, they are two-dimensional representations of a three-dimensional world. It takes a lot of the same mental translation to look at a map and "see" the contours of a lake that it takes to look at a sonar display and "see" the underwater world.

Visualizing Contours

Holy cow! Look at all those lines! Many people look at lake maps. Few understand them.

When you look at a lake map, what do you see? It's not a psychological test; if you see two cats fighting, or a white-winged sparrow, back away and try again.

See the lines for what they are, a rough sketch of the bottom contours of a body of water. Try this, for starters: Look at the shallowest contour line (the one closest to shore). It should go all the way around the lake. Look at the distance between the shoreline and the first contour line.

In your mind, step off the bank and walk out to that first line. If you're 6 feet tall, the water is now up to your shoulders! That's not a line on a map any more; it's the 5-foot contour.

Make a mental trip all the way around that 5-foot line. Notice that (at least on most maps) it's close to shore in some places, farther away in others. Where the line is farther from shore, it stays shallow longer. You could walk out a long way. Where it's closer to shore, it's a "steeper break." No matter how long it takes—do this at breakfast for a week if you have to—stick with it until you see the bottom drop off, and mentally "see" 5 feet of water, instead of that line on the map.

At this point, you're farther along than most anglers ever are able to get!

Move out to the next contour line, usually 10 feet. You're probably in a room with 10-foot ceilings. Look up at the ceiling. That's how deep the water is now.

Make another slow trip around the lake map, and things get more interesting. You'll start to see shallow flats and quick drop-offs into deeper water! Go ahead and let your mind wander out to the 15-, 20-, and 25-foot contour lines, assuming your lake gets that deep. Points stick out, and large flats. Shallow bays have a deep hole in them, instead of just another circle on the map.

Upon close inspection, you'll notice that in some places the contour lines drop off (the water gets deeper) to a certain point, then get shallower again. Don't see the lines; see the water drop into a trough and rise onto another flat, or whatever it rises onto. You'll begin to "see" structure, as though somebody emptied all the water from the lake for you! Certain large areas are mostly deep water; others mostly shallow. It's an amazing feeling—the first time you really understand a lake map.

Wow! Now look at all those lines!

What's that? You don't see the lines anymore? You see the rough shape of the lake bottom?

Now we're talkin'.

If this were a Boy Scout or Girl Scout meeting, you'd be asked to get some modeling clay and make a "3D" model of the map you're looking at. Making a clay model can help an angler visualize lake structure.

Using And Fine Tuning Maps

Maps are fun to look at in your basement. But they're most useful out on the water.

After you understand what the contour lines represent, you're ready to use a map to help you find fish. The first time you pull away from the landing, turn on your sonar unit and watch as the depth drops off to 5 feet. You are at the 5-foot contour line. Watch as it drops to 10 feet. Now, you're at the 10-foot line.

It sounds like kindergarten, but most anglers never even get this good at using a lake map.

One thing that complicates matters is that you have to look for other things on your sonar. Is the bottom hard or soft? Is there any weed, timber, brush or other cover? Do you see any baitfish? Any big fish?

At first, concentrate mainly on following the contour lines and "finding" a spot you want to fish. Say you're looking for a major point. Here's one way to find it:

Drive your boat into the vicinity, and motor away from shore into water deeper than the top of the point. Now, run parallel to shore, in a path that will take you over the point. You'll know when you go over the point. Your depthfinder reading will come up, up, up.

You found it!

But hey, wait a minute. It says on the map the top of the point never gets shallower than 10 feet. It's only 5 feet deep here. And look at those rocks! If you would have been a few feet to the side, your motor would have hit them!

You just learned another valuable lesson: Maps aren't

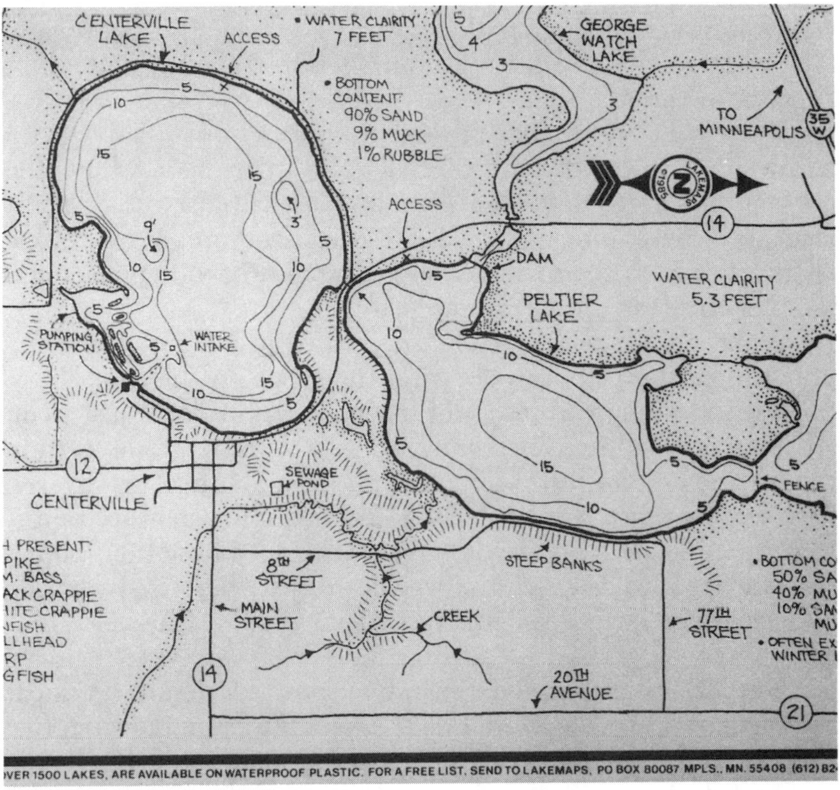
CENTERVILLE LAKE
ACCESS
WATER CLARITY 7 FEET
BOTTOM CONTENT: 90% SAND 9% MUCK 1% RUBBLE
GEORGE WATCH LAKE
TO MINNEAPOLIS
35 W
14
ACCESS
DAM
PELTIER LAKE
WATER CLARITY 5.3 FEET
PUMPING STATION
WATER INTAKE
12
CENTERVILLE
SEWAGE POND
FENCE
PIKE
8TH STREET
MAIN STREET
CREEK
STEEP BANKS
77TH STREET
20TH AVENUE
21
1500 LAKES, ARE AVAILABLE ON WATERPROOF PLASTIC. FOR A FREE LIST, SEND TO LAKEMAPS, PO BOX 80087 MPLS., MN. 55408 (612)

You might not think a contour map is important for fishing "bowl-shaped" lakes. But isn't it a huge headstart just to know the lake's contours are bowl-shaped? Also, better maps provide clues about water clarity, bottom composition, rock piles or other hard-bottomed areas.

perfect. Lake maps are made to help scientists study and manage lakes, not for anglers. They are good basic models of the rough contours of a lake bottom. They are not done in microscopic detail. (Also, it depends on water level conditions the year the map was made. The lake that year may have held more water so that the top of the submerged point was at 10 feet. However, drought and water resource use may have lowered the overall water level in the meantime. Remember, climatic conditions certainly play an important role in determining water levels, and lake water levels are not static.)

So, you have to fine-tune your maps. Now, being careful, go back over the shallow part of that point. Turn and motor down the point, toward deeper water. You'll see it drop off.

When you drop into deep water, turn and come back to

where it starts getting shallow again. Now, pick a depth and follow it. You'll see that the point is not shaped exactly as it appears on the map.

There's a little point, in fact, that sticks out off the main point. It's not on the map. And there's one spot where the bottom goes soft. Better go back and look that over. Hey, it leads into the point, and weeds are thick in there! Wow! None of this stuff is on the map. Better get out a notebook and sketch some of this, for the next time you fish it.

Whether you realize it or not, you've just done something only the best anglers can do: Find the "spot on the spot."

It's not enough to just find the point. Fish don't just swim all over the point. They move up and down along certain routes, and certain little things offer good ambush points to feed from. Sometimes the fish will be shallow on the point, sometimes deeper. But if you have a good idea how the point is really shaped, and where the weeds are, or where that old pile of dead trees is, you can fish those spots before your boat runs over them.

Sure, it takes time to examine spots in detail. A great tournament angler, Mike Schuett, says, "If I fish more than five spots in a day, I know I'm not being thorough enough."

He fishes on a very complex lake, with structures that are hard to visualize. Some lakes, and some spots, are easier to figure out. With experience, you'll know how many spots you can effectively fish, in the amount of time you have.

Lakes Without Much Structure
Granted, certain lakes don't have much "structure" in the classic sense. Some lake basins are "simple."

These are often called bowl-shaped lakes. You might think that maps don't do you much good on these lakes, but isn't it a huge headstart just to know there isn't much classic structure?

On these waters, other things become important. Any weeds? The weed edges, or weedlines, probably hold a lot of fish. Weeds that form a canopy help keep the water under them cooler than exposed water, during midsummer heat spells. Piles of brush and other cover are also possible fish collectors. Even minute changes of depth can be important breaklines with fish.

Changes in bottom density can also hold concentrations of

fish, such as where mud meets sand or gravel. If you're good with your sonar unit, you can find those by running the lake at moderate speed.

Good News: Fishing-Oriented Maps

The good news is that lake maps are becoming more "fishing-oriented" all the time. You can get basic contour maps from public agencies, like local natural resources offices or the Army Corps of Engineers. But more and more private businesses are coming out with maps that have fishing information.

Ask around to find the best maps of your waters. Check with all the best bait shops in your area, and look for ads in local outdoor publications, as many map-makers advertise.

What kind of information do they provide? It varies, but they often list: fish species present, in rough order of abundance; information on bottom content, including some details on the map; the depth at which weeds often stop growing; something about the water clarity, and reason for any staining; some even have detailed write-ups about the lake, and how to fish it in various seasons.

In a hurry? At least one outfit will fax you a map.

How Can Maps Help Shore Anglers?

Anglers who don't own a boat often feel left out by the advancing parade of modern fishing aids. But maps can help.

By looking over a lake map, shore anglers can quickly find spots where deep water cuts close to shore. They can see places where "complex" structural areas are within casting, or wading-and-casting, distance. In most cases, these types of spots will produce more consistent fishing, and bigger fish, than huge expanses of shallow water.

There are exceptions, such as during early spring and spawning periods, when large shallow areas often hold numbers of adult gamefish. But for consistent shore-fishing action, it's hard to beat a spot where "deep water comes close to the bank."

7

Visualizing Structure In Lakes And Reservoirs

K nowing and locating the temperatures fish seek reduces your search for productive water in lakes to a small fraction of the whole. Now, let's reduce it even further, eliminating perhaps 95 percent. The other five percent is where most of the fish are.

The elimination of unproductive water has to do with the structure of lakes. "Structure fishing" is the system of studying the underwater habitats of fish to determine where to find most of them. Expert anglers have always understood structure fishing to some extent, but the use of sonar and temperature probes has taken a lot of guess work out of the game. It has been said that you can find structure without fish, but you can't find fish without structure. While this isn't always true, as many species tend to suspend in mid-range depths, it is true often enough that it deserves further study.

Underwater structure that harbor fish are of two kinds—natural and man-made. The latter are usually found in artificial lakes and reservoirs. Some structure is visible on or from the surface, or can be deduced by land characteristics, such as a creek channel, a deep ditch or a small valley going into a lake, or a point of land. Other structure, being much deeper, can only be located by sonar.

Streambeds

Channels of streams often extend far out into lakes or

When fishing newly formed impoundments, one of the best starting points is working the old river channel. In this case, it also means working a drop-off where the vertical rock face protrudes well above water level.

reservoirs, usually dispersing into their depths. When lakes have been raised by dams or have been created as impoundments, these channels are usually long and distinct. Impoundments are often made by dams raised over riverbeds. In this case, the main channel usually extends the entire length of the impoundment with vein-like smaller channels of what formerly were tributary streams and brooks. All of these are structure which may harbor fish, but parts of them are much better.

One place is where the former streambed (now deeply hidden in the lake) makes a sharp bend, forming a deep hole on the outside. These holes are important fish-holding structure. Another is the junction where a smaller stream joins a bigger one. The deep holes usually found at such junctions can also be important fish-holding structure.

Visualizing Structure In Lakes And Reservoirs   79

Maps made of the area before it became an impoundment show these streams and their characteristics. If such a map is contoured, the shape of the impoundment can be drawn in. Actual locations can be estimated by sightings of landmarks above the surface. Sonar can pinpoint them more exactly.

Such channels often act as migratory routes between holding areas in deep water and feeding areas in the shallows, but more about that later. You know that water temperatures have a distinct influence on fish and how they use these routes, and that temperatures vary from season to season.

Deep Holes And Migratory Routes

As said before, contour maps of lakes often show holes of varying size and depth caused by topographical adjustments not associated with channels. When these holes have hard bottoms, and when the water there contains sufficient oxygen and is of suitable temperature, they can be valuable holding areas for fish. Well-equipped anglers can easily locate these holes with their sonar and determine if they hold fish. If a hole doesn't produce, mark it down for a later attempt, and move on to other structure.

When water in deep holes is of proper temperature and contains sufficient oxygen, the holes can be suitable bedrooms for fish, but they may be inadequate as dining rooms. Fish rest comfortably there, but they have to migrate to less comfortable and perhaps more exposed places to feed. Thus, they establish migratory routes between resting and feeding spots which, in the case of largemouth bass, for example, may be in grassy or weedy areas in shallows close to shore. Other fish, such as trout, may prefer to feed on reefs or bars. In either case, the migratory route usually is the easiest way to travel from place to place—a streambed, a gully or a gradual slope rather than a steep one. Contour maps may indicate probable migratory routes. Fish going into shallows to feed usually take these routes in late afternoon, returning when they have fed, or as late as early the next morning. Anglers fishing these routes at proper times are often very successful.

Points Of Land

Easy-to-locate points of land which drop off quickly are my

How To Fish a Point of Land

Although the hotspot when fishing a point of land is usually off the tip, it pays to cover all the water by fan-casting from position 1 and working around to position 5. Anchor the boat at each position and cover the water thoroughly.

favorite starting spots. Depth can be estimated by the steepness of the point before moving on with your sonar. Many kinds of gamefish common to the lake, especially trout, walleyes and bass, are found in such places when water temperature is suitable, because water around points also provides the other requirements of fish—a food supply if the point is grassy or bushy, the protection of vegetation and dark or shaded water, and abundant oxygen. Hotspots usually are off the tips of points. The shady side should be the better one, but it usually pays to explore the whole point thoroughly.

This is usually done by fancasting from enough anchored positions to cover the entire point, both on or near the surface and bottom, as indicated in the sketch. It can be done from a slowly moving boat if you are in a hurry, but this may not allow enough time to fish the bottom properly. Keep the boat at a distance that allows you to cast lures safely into the grasses or bushes. If a hang-up occurs and you can't pull loose, consider breaking off the lure rather than going to get it—and spooking the fish. It can most likely be retrieved after the area has been fished.

Noises alarm fish, and a hotspot may seem barren after someone has tossed out the anchor or banged a tackle box. Consider the advantage of a quiet, electric motor. Lower the anchor carefully. And try putting a springy rug on the boat's deck to deaden sounds made by feet and equipment.

Water temperature tells us whether to fish near surface or down deep. In early morning and late evening, the surface may be productive anyway. If not, depth is the answer. My first choice then might be to cast a plastic worm to shore and to walk or hop it very slowly down the incline until it is under the boat. Spinnerbaits, jigs, spoons and bottom-scratching lures also pay off from time to time. Everyone has their favorite types of lures in choices of sizes and colors, but opinions advanced by experts will be discussed later in this book.

When steep-breaking structure is nearby and when points of land contain considerable surface and subsurface vegetation (with its accompanying food supply), places like this can be especially productive.

Drop-Offs To Deep Water

The closeness of surface and subsurface contour lines on topographical maps indicates how fast the bottom drops off. This can also be determined by observing where a cliff shelves steeply into the water. Topographical maps showing subsurface contours often reveal unseen drop-offs which may be even better than the others.

Drop-offs extending down steeply from the surface are especially good when wind or a breeze blows toward them. When surface water is colder than fish prefer, but when the day is warm, the surface water will heat up and the wind will blow this warmer top water toward the drop-off—in effect, piling it up. The surface water there can be several degrees warmer than the rest of the lake, making it a sought-after place for fish.

Winds also blow surface foods toward the drop-off. These

Complete Angler's Library

foods may be spent insects and other small things, but they attract baitfish, which in turn attract gamefish. For these reasons drop-offs can be very productive in the colder weather of early or late season.

A drop-off is typical of many hotspots in lakes. At the shoreline the point drops off into 6 to 8 feet of water and then gently slopes toward the deeper part of the lake and the channel of the incoming stream at the left. This rock and gravel slope is ideal habitat for many species of fish but particularly for smallmouth bass and trout.

You could fish this point from a boat anchored or drifting as far out as possible, casting in to the rocks, and then working the lure down the incline. You also could cast from shore, give the lure plenty of time to sink on a loose line, and then work it in close to the bottom up the incline. If smallmouth bass are presumed to be in this location, a 3-inch weighted plastic worm or ½-ounce jig might do well if hopped up or down the incline very slowly. Spinners or spoons should be productive for trout. When water temperatures tempt fish to the top, streamers or bucktails should do well in sizes and colors imitating prevalent baitfish.

Coves And Thoroughfares

A thoroughfare is an almost currentless, river-like passage from one lake to another. For example, the outlet of a higher lake entered a lower lake, but the damming of the lower lake to make a reservoir has brought both lakes to the same level. The original streambed has been greatly deepened by the flooding to provide an interesting fish-holding structure.

Because this is a migratory route from one lake to the other, both baitfish and gamefish collect in this spot. In late spring and early fall, fish will travel the thoroughfare in search of better water temperatures or better spawning locations, often tarrying at this junction before passing through. The steep banks may be weedy and abundant with food. A bridge offers shade and protection from its pilings for fish.

Anglers fishing off the bridge or near its abutments might not realize how deep the water is. They probably would try lures near the surface and then fish them a bit deeper, not realizing that their quarry would be holding or feeding close to the bottom. The trick is to cast far out and to feel bottom while working in the lure. To get the lure down after making the cast, do not put the line back under control of the reel. Let line peel off freely so the lure will sink directly to the bottom instead of reeling it in on a tight line. Each cast should explore the bottom in this manner. When line stops peeling off, put it under control of the reel and fish it along the bottom.

Now, assume that this bridge crosses a narrow arm of the lake which goes into a weedy cove. The width of the cove makes no difference; all coves are worth investigating, particularly when winds make the lake too rough for fishing.

If the cove is rich in weeds, grasses and pads, and therefore abundant in food, gamefish from the lake will often come in to feed. When water temperatures are to their liking in the cove, or perhaps when surface waters grow cooler in evening or early morning, the normal piscatorial population of the cove will be augmented by visitors from the lake, many of which may be of trophy size. The cove may be a hotspot for pike, or for largemouth or smallmouth bass—or for many other species when conditions are right. Catfish and their kin may be there all the time, as well as walleyes, crappies, bluegills, pike and other types of fish.

Submerged Islands, Reefs And Bars

Regardless of depth, structure protruding from a lake's bottom—submerged islands, reefs and bars—almost always produce fish. Some structure may be observed by peering into a lake through polarized glasses. Others may be discerned by a rock or two breaking the surface, or by vegetation near the surface. If a point of land extends toward an island, a bar probably runs part way between.

Most submerged structure, however, can't be located on the surface. They can be located accurately by sonar, which tells how deep the summit of the structure is, how far it protrudes above the bottom, whether the structure is muddy or hard, and how thick the vegetation is, as well as the presence or absence of fish. With a contour map and sonar, you can quickly learn all about the bottom structure of a lake.

You now know how to find the correct temperature depth for the species of fish you seek. The idea is to fish close to

Marker buoys such as this commercially produced buoy usually can be made out of plastic or Styrofoam and are handy for marking fish-holding areas when you find them so you can stay on them.

bottom structure at the right depth, because fish will be lying or cruising close to them for protection and food. Contours can be marked to identify correct paths for trolling. Temperature readings tell you where to anchor and how deep to fish to hit bottom at proper levels.

Surface markers are valuable for this, and they can be made or purchased. One type is shaped like a dumbbell and made of a brightly colored, floatable material with line wound around its waist and a weight at the end of the line. When your probing tells you that you are over the right spot to hit bottom at the right depth, you drop one of these markers. The weight quickly unwinds the line and hits bottom. Then, the line is half-hitched around the marker. In fishing a reef, several of these may be dropped to mark its length. Then, you can drift or

Visualizing Structure In Lakes And Reservoirs

troll over the area and always know we are on the right path.

When the tops of these structures (sometimes called "mounds") are at suitable temperature depth, fish may roam and feed over them, particularly when these mounds are covered with aquatic growth. Weedy tops of relatively shallow structure are hotspots for yellow perch. Smallmouth bass hold on tops or sides of rocky or gravel structure at suitable temperature depth. Largemouth bass prefer hard bottoms.

Weedy And Grassy Areas

Pond and lake shallows which are thick with lily pads, hyacinths, grasses and weeds offer protection and food for fish.

Weedbeds, lily pads and grassy areas are an ideal habitat for largemouth bass, bluegills and other fish; also for trout when water temperatures are agreeable to them. Largemouth bass spawn in such places in the spring, sweeping out circular depressions between the growths to expose gravel on which they lay their eggs. When the shallow water becomes too warm in summer, the bass leave these areas for deeper water, but they may return daily at dusk to feed and remain perhaps until sunup the next day.

Since weedy areas often have few open spots, you have the choice of casting weedless lures at random and working them over the pads or of fishing the weedline, which probably will be more productive and more fun. Here's a tip on fishing weedlines like this:

Wade if possible, but use a silent boat if not. Cast as close as possible to the weedline and fish the lure in along the edge. Make the first cast short, gradually extending the length of subsequent casts. This procedure hooks the nearest fish without alarming those farther away.

More fish usually lie along the weedline rather than amidst the growth inside of it, but if the inside has open holes, or if there are open-water cuts entering the growth from the weedline, these can be hotspots and should be fished carefully. The firm edge of weeds sometimes indicates that there may be a drop-off along it. This would make fishing even better.

Anglers from all over North America travel to Florida to fish for big bass. The sport is a way of life for fishermen near the Everglades National Park. Whether or not you've been there, or may ever want to go there, this unusual sort of largemouth bass fishing is packed with thrills and challenges.

The "sea of grass" in the Everglades can be explored in part by following boat trails, but airboats are needed to reach remote areas. Don't venture far from civilization without an expert guide because it's easy to get lost.

Anglers sometimes leave their airboat and wade from open pocket to open pocket, carefully covering each one with various lures in search of big bass. Light johnboats are used wherever there are canals or boat trails. "Reading the water" usually means "reading the grass," finding potholes and other fairly open places where one can cast without getting snagged too often. When fishing narrow canals and boat trails, anglers usually cast straight ahead, covering both sides as near the grass as possible. Bass lie in the edges of the grass ready to pounce on moving bait.

Another interesting kind of Southern fishing is casting for bass in flooded cypress forests or swamps. Gamefish forage in the inundated areas, which would contain no water in dry weather. When swamps are draining, the gamefish and baitfish are forced to leave, so these are the times to fish the outlet drainage canals.

Man-Made Structure

Impoundments created for flood control and for reservoirs are often many miles long with arms and bays which once were lowlands and valleys. In flooding the area, it may have been necessary to cover towns, villages and farms, as well as wooded lands. The result is a complex of man-made structure which become havens for fish and hotspots for fishermen. In shallow areas, some of this structure can be seen from the surface. Most of it, however, is deep and must be located by maps or with the use of sonar.

Old maps of the area, made before the impoundment was created, can be used by marking the contour of the water level. This reveals the present shape of the impoundment and all that is submerged in it. Geological Survey maps may or may not show these details, but anglers can make such maps if regional sources don't provide them.

While fishing submerged roadbeds, it's best to look around.

A good map will show the direction of the submerged road and the various structure it weaves through. Focus your efforts in the areas that hold the species you're after. For example, smallmouth will hold in areas with medium to large rocks because their favorite forage, crayfish, frequents these areas. Walleyes, too, may be found in these areas, but they may also be suspended over a deep, feeding flat near the roadway. A deep cut, on the other hand, is ideal for largemouth bass, so try trolling over the cut or casting crankbaits.

Causeways

A causeway is a raised road—for example, a road built on fill along a river or over a swampland. Causeways are often productive structure for bass, walleyes and other gamefish.

Say your map shows that a typical causeway runs along the river. In this instance, it probably can be traced by the elevation of ground above lake level, part of which was bulldozed to make the road. The road and the streambed both are excellent structures for trolling or casting, but the most productive parts of the streambed are the deeper outside curves.

The road may run across a depression which had to be filled in to make a complete causeway, and this may contain a bridge or two, which should be indicated on the map. The low area on each side of the causeway could provide excellent fishing.

One might say that this is a rather extensive area to fish. Some parts of the area should be better than others, but even the poorest parts offer better structure than most of the impoundment. Many anglers say that only about five percent of a natural lake or an impoundment is worth fishing. The important thing is trying to identify the various types of structure that make up that important five percent, so the rest can be ignored.

Rock-Fill

Rock-fill is used to support causeways, such as riprapping along the bank of a stream. Such rocky places are havens for baitfish, since they provide shade, protection and food. Rock-fill becomes crayfish habitat. At sundown, crayfish crawl from their hideouts in the underwater rocks to forage the lake bottom for food. Gamefish should be nearby. Crankbaits or jigs

Riprap used to shore up banks of streams and sometimes on lakes or reservoirs serves as a home for crayfish which in turn attract baitfish and then gamefish.

imitating crayfish (or baitfish) should bring strikes, and casts should be made as close as possible to the rocks, which may harbor large fish in their crevices.

Fishing may not be allowed near dams in reservoirs, but if so, the dam may be a hotspot. While exploring dammed impoundments, it often pays to drop a temperature probe near the dam. Jigging or baitfishing at the right temperature depth should produce results. A sonar unit will help you pinpoint breaks and fish.

Standing Timber And Brush

In certain parts of the country, anglers refer to underwater mazes of brush and timber as "stump ranches" or "stick-ups." They are usually found in man-made lakes that have been created by damming creek channels. These areas are dynamite for bass, crappies and walleyes. Rainbow and brown trout also gravitate to this type of cover because it contains an abundance of minnows and large aquatic insects.

This is ideal water for using fly-rod popper bugs for panfish and largemouth bass. It also is excellent for live bait such as minnows or hellgrammites fished just off the bottom on a small bobber. When streamer flies or nymphs are fished deep, the barbs should be protected with looped monofilament weed guards. Casts should be directed to the open spots that are close to the stumps.

A similar structural situation is offered by brush piles, which are prevalent in many Southern lakes. In fishing Lake Ouachita, in Arkansas, crappies and bass were most prevalent in two places—off grassy points of land and near brush piles. The brush was rooted to the bottom which was 10 feet deep.

A Review Of Deep Structure Fishing

The following six points summarize the procedure for finding fish in deep water.

1. Use a hydrographic (depth contour) map to identify potential fish-holding areas—and learn how to read it (see Chapter 6).

In doing these two things, you have immediately eliminated at least 90 percent of the lake, so you don't need to waste time with it. Confine your fishing to a definite depth, and to only a few places (or trolling paths) at that depth.

In selecting bottom structure, remember that it may contain substructure, which narrows down the presumed hotspots even more. What is substructure? It is the best part of the structure. Here are three examples: If the structure is a submerged streambed, its substructure would be the sharp bends in it, and particularly the deeper outside curve of the bends. If the structure is a mass of standing dead timber or heavy brush, its substructure would be open places in it. If the structure is a submerged roadbed, its substructure would be the ditches that lay beside it.

2. Use sonar to find the general areas you've identified on the map, and to "hone" in for more detail. Once found, spend a few minutes searching the structure for the presence of fish. If none are found, move to the next area on the map.

3. Fish the selected structure only long enough to determine their productiveness, because fish from time to time prefer one type of structure to another. If a structure is unproductive, don't waste time with it.

Some structure may be unsuitable for fish because of oxygen deficiency—for example, the lower level of a stratified reservoir. In oxygen-deficient areas, there may be places where there is an oxygen inversion—an area in the deficient part which contains sufficient oxygen. Pay specific attention to the rules of thermocline.

4. When a good structure is found, concentrate on others that are similar. For example, if the fish are in curves in a submerged streambed or in open spots in masses of standing timber, concentrate on these to the exclusion of other places. The fish are following a pattern—a similar environment of temperature, oxygen, cover and food, and you should fish the pattern. Some patterns may be productive for several days. When they cease producing, you must start over.

Structure fishing is easier now because of the help sonar provides. But it is still easy to do things wrong. This book will help you avoid the pitfalls. Reread and absorb the information in this book, then apply what you learn to specific situations. This takes time and thought and planning. You may have to try a variety of structure before finding a pattern or patterns that will pay off most of the time.

8

Locating Hotspots in Rivers

N
ow, the various types of water found in most rivers and the ability to fish them will be discussed in greater detail. This chapter refers mainly to the various species of trout, but will also consider smallmouth bass, walleyes and other species. All of them seek fairly similar holding and feeding positions.

The photographs that accompany this chapter were taken on fishing rivers showing typical holding or feeding positions that are considered to be "hotspots." This means that the positions are known to hold fish.

Holding Water And Feeding Water

Two kinds of water are shown: *holding water* where fish usually lie or rest during travel because it offers moderate flow plus the protection of obstructions, depth and the concealment of a disturbed surface; and *feeding water* where fish can usually be seen in riffles, eddies, shallow parts of a gravel pool, feed lanes, or areas under bushy banks where food drops down to them. Feeding water, of course, is productive only during feeding periods.

These two kinds of water often offer characteristics that combine to make certain places both holding and feeding water. Usually, these spots provide moderate flow and protection in the close proximity of a feed lane or other access to food such as overgrowth overhead. When both conditions are satisfied, these places should be best of all.

Not shown, of course, are the majority of areas in rivers which do not satisfy these conditions and where gamefish have no reason to be. These include thin, flat stretches offering little or no concealment and widely scattered food supply; areas with muddy or sandy bottom (without concealment and with less than minimal food supply); and backwaters which contain little or no current.

In reading water, anglers new to an area should take time before fishing it to study the rocks, edges, runs, feed lanes and deep holes which combine to make up the structure of a river. Spent insects, leaves and other bits of debris drifting downstream mark feed lanes; rocks or other obstructions in these lanes should be noted as possible hotspots. Holding positions inside edges should be noted. "If I were a trout, where would I prefer to be?" is the question to be answered. At first, such study takes a bit of time, but the experienced water reader can size up situations at a glance. While you can't catch fish unless your lure is in the water, it pays to devote a few minutes to making the rest of the time more productive.

Since you're not at the river, this chapter will try to bring interesting spots to you by analyzing the photographs which follow. It pays to study them. They will be similar to many spots on rivers that you fish.

Edges Formed By Partially Submerged Rocks

Looking downstream in this picture, you can see a good-looking shale and gravel bottom from which several fairly large rocks emerge. The moderate flow around the nearest rock may be too shallow to interest fish. This depends on the river's height and the amount of protection afforded.

The next rock, to the right, is in much deeper water, with wide edges and a large submerged rock to its right, both combining to make a small feed lane between them. A fairly large trout lies inside the edge in the feed lane, and two others lie in the moderate flow area near the rock's left edge.

Just downstream of this left edge is a small edge made by a submerged rock. A deep hole to the right of this is where a trout can feed because it is also in the tail of the big edge, the two combining to form a small feeding lane.

Farther downstream, at top left of the picture, a rock forms another wide edge. (The one to the left of it, like the first one discussed, probably is in water too shallow to be of interest.) A trout lies in the wide right edge, which brings up the point that, when a rock forms two edges, the deeper one near midstream usually is the better one.

After fishing these edges, you should try another cast or two before moving on. Note that the right edges of the two deepest rocks tend to converge. This may mean that there is a small, deep channel there, and the combination also indicates a feed lane, so this is a good spot to try. Casts should be swung or drifted upstream of this spot and then extended farther downstream.

Complex Lies Above And Below Stream Rocks

Note a rather deep riverbed channel flowing in to the lower right portion of the picture. Several large rocks lie near the middle of the channel just below the center of the picture. The "V" made by the edges of a submerged rock can be seen clearly in the white water below the rock that emerges. A rather indistinct edge is made by the smaller rock at the upper right of

Complete Angler's Library

the emerging one, but the quiet water it forms indicates this.

Brown trout commonly select a lie behind a rock formation like this. If a rainbow trout was in the area, it probably would lie in the faster water of the channel just upstream of the "V," in the protection of this deep stretch, because rainbows usually prefer faster water than brown trout. If the river contained steelhead during a run, a fish probably would lie in the spot from which the brown trout was taken, or in the deep but protected area of white water near the center of the picture.

This deep depression, which has been gouged out around the spot at top right, is a good spot for big trout of all species. The flow near the streambed is moderate because of depth and large rocks there. The lie also is protected by the disturbed surface. Anglers would first fish the near channel from a concealed position farther back, paying particular attention to the spot between the legs of the white-water "V." Then, they should extend their casts to work their lure through the nearby depression.

Fishing A Large Eddy

This is a situation where the right tactics should raise a lunker or two—probably trophy brown trout. Sit on a rock, well below the eddy, and try to read what is going on.

The river flows from top right to lower left, riffling down from the pool above. The riffle shelves from the gravel bank at upper left toward the big boulder, which breaks the fast flow of the stream here to make a large, swirling eddy moving in a counterclockwise direction. A pronounced edge extends from the rock's tip downstream just to the left of the long slick caused by the big boulder and subsurface rocks. Other slicks and churning current indicate more large subsurface rocks, providing excellent holding positions for several trophy-sized fish. Just to the left of the edge the main force of the current is compressed to provide a feed lane, so the fish holding don't have to travel far for food. The rocks also are sure to harbor schools of minnows that attract predator fish.

The trout will probably follow the normal pattern of lying in the moderate flow just inside the edge, but since the water is rather turbulent, they should be deep, behind subsurface rocks. An upstream cast to the boulder's point, into the foam, allows the lure to run deep, but line must be retrieved rapidly to keep it fairly tight in order to feel strikes. The lure should be fished all the way to the extreme left of the picture, and several casts should be made in order to fish the edge thoroughly.

Casts more inside the edge should then cause the lure to sweep in the counterclockwise direction of the eddy. Every attempt should be made to fish the lure deep. Bucktails or streamers on a floating line with a sinking tip, or perhaps weighted nymphs, should help fly fishermen to connect. If weighted lures are being used, they should be compact spoons.

Note that the riffling shelves off deeply. Fish may be holding in the deep water just to the right of this area, perhaps resting in this position preparatory to combating the fast water of the riffle on their upstream journey. Casts should be made to the upper part of the deep water so the lure will sink and swing down through the "V" of the current and also deeply through the deep-water area.

Fishing A Deep Hole

Deep holes offer several opportunities for finding fish, and you can assume there are some big ones. The river is split by a riffle, which divides it into the main channel and a secondary one where it shelves off steeply into the deep hole. You can see the faint edge extending downstream from the grassy point, marked by the line of bits of foam and floating debris. Note that this line curves counterclockwise to form a wide and deep eddy.

Experience says that fish can be expected in several positions in a situation like this. There is a deep hole on the other side of the point. Most of the fish will be lying in deep water on the side of the point that is in the shade. During midday on this side of the point they should be hugging bottom, along the edge caused by the point, or under the drop-off. Lures must dredge the bottom.

Probably the best times to fish a deep hole like this are during daybreak and after dusk, when the hole's inhabitants

lose some of their caution and roam the pool for food. Then, and particularly when an insect hatch is on, dry flies should furnish good sport, and the lack of conflicting currents indicates that long floats are possible. If lacking a hatch, weighted nymphs should do the trick because the gravel should be alive with the naturals. Streamers or bucktails, matched in size, shape and color to prevalent baitfish, should do well, too, particularly when stripped in fairly fast after allowing them to sink deeply. This spot is also a good one for spinners and spoons. If the river contains smallmouth bass, you should find some good ones here.

Riffles Below An Island

Islands in moderate or fast-flowing rivers form current edges on their downstream sides. In this situation, you have a pointed island in a fast river, producing a distinct edge with the main flow on this side of the island. On the far side of the island is a slow, deep riffle combining with the fast, shallow one on the side with the main flow. Fish should be lying along the edge on the slow, deep side.

The small outcropping extending into the upper right of the picture causes a secondary edge to flow into the lip of a pool. Fish should be lying in the more moderate flow on the near side of the edge, and the hotspot for them should be just over the lip where the water deepens into the pool.

The nearest edge is probably of minor importance, but darker water on the downstream part of it indicates depth, so it is worth a try even though fish there will probably be smaller. Probability of success is increased because disturbed water in the lower left of the picture indicates there are rocks there which probably rolled down during a freshet.

This is good water for trout, including steelhead, and also for salmon. A hatch of mayflies would tempt an angler to use dry flies if the water is warmer than 50 degrees, but they must be good floaters.

Eroded Riffles And Edges

This interesting stretch of river offers several fish-finding clues. At the top of the picture are eroded gravel riffles which have been broken down in their centers to form ridges on each side and a short pool or run in between. If the water in the pools or runs is deep enough, and especially if it contains rocks, it may offer good cover for fish. If not, this may be a good feeding area, only a short distance from the protective cover of overgrowth at the top of the picture. During mayfly hatching activity the trout would feed here, usually at dusk, on adult mayflies and nymphs.

Just below the riffle there are curved edges made by a large submerged rock. If there is a lunker in the pool, this should be his home.

The water in the foreground is relatively shallow, but rocks which have rolled downstream have been deposited at the edge of the faster flow, where the current deepens. The disturbed surface indicates many subsurface rocks which slow during the flow along the river's bottom, making this a likely holding and feeding area for trout.

Gamefish, when not actively feeding on or near the surface, lie in the protective cover of rocks on the bottom in a location

Complete Angler's Library

like this. Bouncing the bottom with your lures should be done, especially when the water is cold. If the lure isn't felt to touch bottom periodically, you aren't fishing deep enough. Getting hung up occasionally and losing a lure or two may be bothersome, but it pays off with more and bigger fish!

Edges And Lies Formed By Debris

These wooded pools were approached when a rise of trout was in progress, and the actual positions of several of them were noted. These fish weren't very big, but taking a few on drifting dry flies is what makes angling a cherished sport.

The big tree, which drifted downstream during high water, lodged near the head of this little pool (upper right) in about 3 feet of water. Other drifting branches and logs have tangled with it to make an area of moderate flow which is an excellent sanctuary for trout. The edge curving between root and trunk also is a feed lane, and a fly drifted down it should attract the two fish indicated by the symbols. Another feed lane and edge flows beside the main trunk, under which several trout should lie. The object is to work lures very close to the trunk so they will be in easy reach of fish lying in the shade below it. Other

fish are out in the pools, actively feeding, and have not been disturbed by the anglers' slow, cautious approach.

Since these pools aren't very deep, artificial flies or nymphs should be better, and offer more sport, than hardware. Dry flies or nymphs are the answer when trout are feeding like this. Drifting nymphs always should be effective in this gravel stream. When no rises are noticed, either nymphs or very small streamers or bucktails, actively stripped in quite deep, should bring strikes.

A Long Pool With Submerged Boulders

This pool is similar to others which have been noted. (It is a common type distinguished by slowly moving water in which the small edges of submerged rocks are clearly visible.) Water in summer is cooled by a fast-flowing inlet stream which enters the pool below the bridge around the river's bend, which is out of view. This is an ideal area for either smallmouth bass or trout.

Some of the probable lies for trout show that all of the little edges and swirls caused by submerged rocks are good holding spots. Of course, the pool would be fished from the left bank toward the right. It may be better to wade deeply into the pool, keeping your silhouette low, working slowly down the pool and

Complete Angler's Library

handling a fairly long line to disturb the trout as little as possible.

Except for the rocks, all of the pool is fairly fine gravel, which indicates that nymphs, fished slowly, are preferred unless the rises of feeding fish suggest using dry flies. If spoons or spinners are used they should be small ones, cast to the right bank and allowed to swing in the slight current before being fished in. Small streamers or bucktails in colors simulating prevalent baitfish should also do well when handled in this manner, with added action being imparted by the rodtip. Fly fishermen that are using submerged attractors should find a floating line with sinking tip and a long, light tapered leader which is ideal for the purpose.

Steep Bank With Obstructions

In this section of the river, the steep bank has been eroded over many years by seasonal high water, causing trees to slide down and obstruct the current. Although there are no rocks to make edges and holding water, they are formed by other obstructions such as earth slides and fallen trees.

Quickly note that the near side of the stream is slowly shelving and wadable, while the far one is very deep. Anglers fishing this stretch wade the near side and cast to pockets and

into edges formed by obstructions such as the dead tree at right and the trunk extending into the water at left. These obstructions produce a distinct edge on the far side, providing moderate flow for holding water, plus concealment. Also, a nearer edge by the foam line is caused by the slowly shelving water being gouged out deeply by the force of the current.

Lures should be fished deep inside the edges behind obstructions. With fly rods, sinking lines should be used with streamers or bucktails, or steelhead flies when runs are going upstream.

Shallow Run And Rock-Filled Riffle

This photo shows a flat, shallow run flowing into a short, rock-filled midstream riffle. You should be able to visualize rainbow trout feeding on emerging mayfly nymphs.

Here, the edge is indistinct, but one is caused by midstream rocks and is noted primarily by a faint foam line which also is the most pronounced feed lane nearby. The feeding trout would be just inside of this. Others may be feeding near the lip of the run (to the left of the viewer), but this isn't as good a spot, mainly because it lacks good feed lanes.

A Deep, Rock-Filled Run

This shows a deep, rock-filled run which might reveal no distinguishing characteristics to the casual angler unskilled in reading the water. Closer inspection shows a few "trouty" hotspots. The most prominent of these is the underwater rock mass at the upper left which forms wide edges and a moderate flow area between them. This is excellent brown trout water.

Another feature is the rather indistinct edge, also formed by rocks, extending downstream to the right. The force of the current is directed by these into a channel between the two edges. This provides a glide of moderate flow along the left bank extending down to the tree on the left. Anglers habitually use hard-to-sink dry flies on these rivers and take pride in releasing most of the trout they catch.

A Weedy Meadow Stretch

Lime and other minerals dissolved in the waters of mountain rivers, such as the Yellowstone and other rivers elsewhere, encourage dense growths of weeds which are nurseries of food for trout. This river flows through a meadow stretch containing grassy islands. A fairly level gravel bottom contains many hummocks from which sprout weeds that extend to lie on the surface.

In this photograph, some weedy patches are hard to see. An island juts downstream in the middle of the picture. Large edges extend downstream from both sides. Fish lie inside the edges of this relatively weedless area and, since insect hatches occur very often in season, selected trout are easy to locate.

Complete Angler's Library

Steelhead Rivers

Being an Easterner, I have fished for Atlantic salmon more than I have for lake- or sea-run rainbow trout, whose stamina and exceptional fighting ability have earned them the name of "steelhead." On Western angling trips to fabled rivers such as the Deschutes and the Klamath, I have noted a great similarity between the habits of Atlantic salmon and steelhead. Much of what follows, not only applies to Atlantic salmon, but to Pacific salmon as well.

To conserve energy, all anadromous fish in fast water select the easiest way to ascend the river—the path of moderate flow, even if it runs close to shore. These fish also rest in water of moderate flow, such as between the current edges behind rocks, along ledges, or in the depths of cold-water pools. When an impediment to their passage is reached, such as a stretch of long, rough rapids or a waterfall, many of the fish will hold in the first major moderate-flow area below this point, either to regain strength before going up, or to wait for higher water which would make the passage easier.

Atlantic salmon can be taken legally only with artificial flies. Other lures and baits can be used for steelhead, particularly in the winter, but some feel the greatest sport is to seek them with artificial flies in warmer weather.

Let's study a few typical situations:

A Joining Of Currents

You now know that where two currents join, such as below an island or where a stream enters a river, an edge is formed in which fish may lie on the side offering moderate flow or agreeable temperature. The edge shown here is such a place, and the hotspot is along it because the joining currents have formed a deep, boulder-filled run there.

Note also the current line in the foreground. This stretch of deeper and more moderate flow offers fish an easier travel route up through the rapids coming in at the upper center. The current edge is inside an established path of migration upstream. Fish are hooked consistently in these types of locations.

Complete Angler's Library

A Classic Ledgerock Travel Route

Here, a ledge which can be seen entering the river on the far bank extends into the river to turn the upstream rapids into a fairly deep pool. Steelhead habitually go upstream along the far bank and cross in the protection of the ledge to swim the out-of-sight rapids along the deeper and slower right-hand side. When fish are on the move in overcast weather, or between late afternoon and mid-morning, lures fished close to the ledge often enough should bring frequent strikes.

Since you're trying for moving fish, rather than resting ones, the lure and a moving fish must be in the same place at the same time. Sooner or later, however, anglers who keep their fly or lure in the water can be sure a fish swimming through the run will see it.

Steelhead, like other anadromous salmonoids, follow the same age-old travel routes year after year during upstream migrations. Although these travel routes may change somewhat from year to year in streams with gravel or sandy bottoms, due to the scouring of the stream sides during high water, ledges formed by bedrock remain constant, at least during an angler's lifetime. Since the deep water protected by the ledge has moderate flow, this also may be a good holding position for several fish regaining their strength preparatory to the trip up the rapids.

Holding Positions In Rapids

This spot, similar to some of the examples of holding positions for trout, is typical for steelhead also. The photograph shows several deep pockets behind large boulders offering potential resting lies. Positions to the right seem the best ones because several big rocks provide edges between which the stream bottom has been scoured out deeply. Other good locations can be found by other rocks.

Water like this can be fished most effectively with large, colorful steelhead hairwing wet flies on a floating line or a floating line with a sinking tip. Casts should be made quartering down and across stream, first working the fly along the current edges below the rocks and then, on later casts, making it sweep directly through the pockets themselves. When the fly has completed its swing, let it hang downstream and work it actively before fishing it in. Steelhead often follow a fly but may not take it until its action changes.

Polarized sunglasses are a necessity for reading water properly. They cut down or eliminate glare and help anglers locate pockets, determine depth and see fish.

Holding Water In A Deep Run

When large boulders are in a run (even a fast one), the chances are good that they will shelter holding fish.

The trick is to get the fly or lure down deep because the fish lie close to the bottom. The combination of a weighted fly and an extra-fast-sinking line, with the cast made well above the position, should do it, working the deeply sunken fly as close as possible to the edge.

If spinners or spoons are used, they should be compact and fast-sinking. Cast them up and across current and work them close to the bottom near the boulders.

In bottom dredging there is an axiom that if you don't lose a lure or get hung up occasionally, you're not fishing deep enough. Summer steelhead are more active than winter steelhead, and will move farther for the fly or lure. The cold water makes winter steelhead sluggish, so they hug bottom and won't move very far to take a lure or bait. Baits are very popular for winter-run fish; usually salmon eggs or salmon-egg clusters. Experts roll and bounce these along the bottom and can feel them ticking bottom as they are carried downstream. Pencil leads on light droppers that break lose when stuck work well when bottom-bouncing for winter steelhead.

A Travel Route Up A Classic Glide

By now you should be able to read this glide merely by glancing at it. The current on the near side is deeper and more moderate than on the far side, with a definite edge, separating the two. Steelhead traveling routes such as this normally go up close to the outside edge of the main thrust of the current. Large boulders, indicated by the slicks, may hold fish.

This glide would be fished by wading down the left side of the river if casts to the right bank can be made from there. In such an exposed area, fishing should be best on a bright day early in the morning or after dusk. On overcast days it may be good around noon. Of course, lures must be fished deep, and you should feel them making contact with rocks on the bottom.

Complete Angler's Library

Fish The Shady Side

This chapter ends with an important lesson. The angler
would drift a dry fly down the run close to the far bank. The
point being made is that, when other conditions are compatible, it is better to fish the shady side of a stream than the sunny
side. Trout will travel far to seek shade because it offers comfort
and concealment.

Big trees and smaller bushes overhang the shady side, so
terrestrial insects and other foods will drop in the water. The
water is deep and of moderate flow. The rocks on the bank hold
other food. The place has all the earmarks of a hotspot.

9

Trout Honeyholes of Streams and Brooks

While many anglers prefer the challenges of big rivers and the comparatively bigger fish usually found in them, at least as many seek the fascinating mysteries of smaller streams and brooks. Many prefer the challenges of smaller waters; they are ever-changing, testing an angler's skill and strategy at every bend. Big trout lurk in protected areas down their courses, but if you disturb the surface with poor casts, or show yourself, or make noise, you never see them except as fleeing shadows. The choice of fly is important, but even more so is proper presentation and knowing where to cast. That is what this chapter is about.

A Pool Below A Waterfall

Small dams and waterfalls fascinate anglers, particularly those new at the game, partly because of their beauty but mainly because they think the well-aerated depths beneath them hold the biggest lunkers in the stream. Even if this is so, chances are that the big ones spend daylight hours in unreachable recesses behind the waterfall and only venture into the pool itself late in the day or at night in search of food.

If you can sneak up behind the boulders in the picture's foreground and flick a fly into the little pocket at the top of the edge, you could get an immediate strike from the base of the main waterfall. The edge of the white water can be an ideal lie

for a feeding trout. And, if there is one, there could be more.

The fly would then drift down along the edge to tempt a trout in the deep pocket behind the angler. Other short casts should be made to the pocket under the overhanging rock at left and into the little edge made by the smaller cascade in the middle of the picture. A weighted nymph should be fished close to the pool's bottom. In clement weather, and particularly when the pool is in shade, feeding trout should hit lures solidly and instantly. The fast water doesn't allow them much time to make a decision!

A Pool Under A Rock Face

The current flows in over the riffle at the left, forcefully strikes the ledge and is diverted downstream to the right. Note that the gravel bottom in the foreground extends halfway across the stream, where it drops steeply because the current has gouged it out there. The deep water along the cliff face provides excellent lies for some of the biggest fish.

After striking the ledge, part of the current is forced into a large eddy. The downstream edge of this eddy is a good lie for a big trout. The rest of the current joins that from the eddy to form a smooth pool which is about 8 feet deep. One or more big trout should inhabit this pool, probably very close to the rock. The cliff face is in deep shadow except for a short time at midday, thus giving the fish a sense of security.

Except when insects are hatching and fish are seen to be taking them on the surface, you probably will have to work lures very deep to have them taken in this eddy and pool. Of course, this is a good bait hole if an angler wishes to use lead to get the bait down. Weighted spinners may do the trick, but a small, heavy wobbling spoon should do better. Fly fishermen would choose a weighted nymph on a fast-sinking line. The current will take lures into position, but casts should be made to the cliff face.

Complete Angler's Library

The Tail Of A Long Gravel Pool

This is the end of a long pool with a gravel bottom containing scattered rocks. It empties into a wide riffle which flows into another pool below. The tail of the pool is deeper than you would expect, ranging to almost 3 feet below the submerged rock in the lower foreground. Trout in this pool usually feed on nymphs which cling to rocks on the bottom; otherwise, the fish take the hatching insects on top.

In a gravel pool, most of the trout will be in different positions when they are resting than when they are feeding. Resting positions are indicated where several rocks make edges which are good lies for fish. Other unseen submerged rocks nearer the tail of the pool also may harbor resting fish, and they may be seen rising and feeding from these positions from time to time.

During other periods and especially when major insect hatches occur, usually near dusk in warm weather, feeding trout may drop to the tail of the pool and look for food near the major feed lanes.

There are three major current tongues leaving the pool—one near each bank and one in the middle. Trout on the feed will usually lie in moderate current near the tongues, or feed lanes, and dash out into the faster water from time to time to snatch drifting food.

The best way to fish this pool would be to work upstream using dry flies or nymphs. Spinners such as the Panther Martin and the Mepps should also produce. Cast them out and let them swing on a tight line to cover rocks and current lanes.

Streambed Depressions

This is a familiar situation, a pool emptying over a riffle into a deep depression in the streambed.

Note that submerged boulders, particularly near the lower end of the depression, provide excellent cover for trout. The current edge is clearly marked, but the important edges are caused by rocks on the bottom. The water above the current edge is shallow and worthless.

This stretch should be interesting dry-fly water, and the fish should respond to nymphs. Small streams or bucktails worked around the edges of rocks should produce. Spinners would do better here than spoons because deep-running lures aren't necessary. Dry flies or nymphs should be allowed to follow the current lane. Streamers, bucktails and metal lures can be cast quartering downstream and across and allowed to work edges behind the rocks. Casting can be done from either side, but it would be better to start at the base of the riffle on the far side and to fish down the channel.

Complete Angler's Library

Undercut River Banks

Here is an interesting stretch where the current veers to the left and erodes the bank. Note that all of the thick turf in the middle of the picture has been undercut and has fallen into the stream. When this happens, large slabs of the peaty turf hold together to provide small caves and tunnels under the fallen bank through which part of the stream flows. The banks abound with grasshoppers and grubs, which often drop into the stream; also, large numbers of hatched aquatic insects fall or are blown onto the currents below.

This is an excellent location for trophy brown trout, which lie protected in the coves, edges and tunnels, always ready to dash from cover to snatch food.

The water on this side of the stream's edge holds no promise, so the idea is to work lures as close to the left bank as possible.

I would select a fluffy marabou streamer fly of average size and would fish it upward and downward as close to the bank as possible to provide maximum pulsating action. Why? Because marabou streamers are attractive to big brown trout, especially when they are made to pulsate in one position for a minute or two. Perhaps they look like an enticing new form of food, but they also may incite a big trout to strike out of anger. A light marabou like the Ballou Special is a good choice for a bright day in clear water, but a brown or black one is preferable on an overcast day.

A Tricky Spot

Streams flowing through forested land often present tricky casting problems where downed timber and bushes make accurate lure delivery almost impossible. Casual anglers will glance at such a place and leave it for stretches that are easier. More serious ones will wade downstream slowly and quietly, studying the opportunities, and end up with more fish.

It pays to study the shady edges because trout will lie and feed close to them. It pays to drop a fly or bait into rock-made pockets such as the one in left center.

In addition to edges, pockets, holes and undercut banks, look for sunken masses of dead leaves in the shade. The careful observer may see several trout lying over them, nearly indistinguishable because of their cryptic coloration.

Beaver Ponds

Many streams are dammed by beavers, but the ponds don't always contain trout. We can divide them into two classes. Some, mainly in flat meadows, are more or less stagnant, with insufficient flow to cool the water, and with rotting vegetation caused by water spreading over land areas. A telltale sign of these is the bubbles of marsh gas rising from the muddy bottom due to decomposition. The water lacks sufficient oxygen and is too warm for trout. The other kinds of interest to anglers are ponds created by beavers in flowing streams, usually in hilly country. The current of the cold-water brook keeps the pond cool and properly oxygenated, carrying away contamination of rotting vegetation, which usually is minimal in such places. Trout seek, and thrive in, little ponds like this because they prefer their moderate flow to the faster water of the brooks and because surrounding vegetation provides both food and shade. A pond of this type is shown in the photo. Typical trout lies are easily identified.

Anglers should approach a pond like this from below the dam, using whatever concealment it affords. If no surface feeding is noted, the trick is to use horizontal casts to drop lures as close under the bushes as possible. After that, look the place over for deep, dark holes. Trout may be concentrated in them. Look for evidence of springs trickling in or coming up from the bottom. The best spot may be the inlet where the stream enters the pond.

Small Meadow Brooks

One of my friends enjoys the challenge of meadow brooks so small that he can step across in many places. Several years ago he took me to one, asked me to set up dry-fly tackle with a short leader, and handed me a clipped deer-hair imitation of a bee that he had originated for this kind of fishing. The brook seemed to be no more than a ditch, so small that casting into it would be difficult. Needing instruction and lacking enthusiasm, I lagged behind to watch him.

He dropped to hands and knees at some distance from the brook and wriggled forward as a cat might stalk a mouse. Near the bank he made a short cast, the fly landing on a blade of grass within inches of the water. With a slight twitch he pulled it in—and got an immediate strike from a bright 10-inch brook trout, which he promptly hoisted onto the bank.

Now full of interest at this astonishing trick, I crept to the brook and looked in. Both sides were deeply undercut; the

Small Meadow Brooks

Complete Angler's Library

water was cool and deep, with only a narrow band of sunlight to break the shade on the brook's surface.

"Almost no one bothers with brooks like this," said my friend, "because they don't look like much. Those that do usually spook the trout by noise, or by being seen. Undercut banks act as sounding boards. The trout are shy and the slightest unusual noise will send them to cover. So these fishermen conclude the trout aren't there, and they give up.

"Casting is another problem. You can do it like I did, or use a long rod and merely dap the fly into the brook and let it drift a short distance, or feed the line through the guides and get a longer drift. A short drift usually is all that's necessary.

"Brooks like this always contain small trout because big ones spawn in such places. The best time is late fall when the spawners run up small brooks from rivers and lakes. I only kill males then, and only a very few because I think fishing is for fun rather than for meat.

"Another good time to fish these places," he continued, "is during mid-summer when bigger streams are too warm. Check their temperatures. When they get too warm, the trout come into places like this because of the cooler water. Of course, they also come into more open brooks then. Spinning tackle isn't much good here due to the casting problem. Use a long fly rod with a short, strong leader, and fish either with natural terrestrial baits or their imitations. I prefer my little bees, but grasshoppers or grubs also are good."

=10=

Finding Fish Under The Ice

I t can be a cold, helpless feeling. You're supposed to find fish under parfait layers of ice, slush and snow? Find something that can move at will, while you suffer the handicap of poking and probing through an apparently impassive barrier?

It's no wonder ice fishing is misunderstood.

Most anglers think of ice fishing as a tolerable activity that helps pass time between open-water seasons, when you can really fish. The good news, for the few who have heard it, is that we now have the technology to make ice fishing comfortable and productive. Those are two powerful words that didn't used to mesh with "ice fishing."

Using the same equipment (sonar, lake maps, even loran) and tactics (mobility) we take for granted in summer, you can become efficient on the ice.

More on all this, but for now, picture yourself ...

Stepping into the middle of a crowd of ice anglers. You check how deep the water is, if the bottom is soft or hard, what depth most of the fish are at, and what tactics are working best. Is the spot on, connected to, near, or far from major structural elements? Are there similar spots elsewhere on the lake, or on a nearby lake, that might hold fish? What other types of spots might have fish? Given the time of year, might the fish be moving somewhere else? You know how to find "open areas" among the crowd, and to fish the fringes, where spooked fish may have gone for security.

Using a system that stresses electronics and mobility, you can really fish, despite the coating of ice between you and the quarry you seek.

Ice Fishing's "Seasons"

Fish location changes from spring through summer, fall and winter, a fact many anglers already understand. But did you realize fish location—and feeding moods—often also change under the ice, from early to late winter?

In their "search" for fish under ice, most people simply go where they see others fishing. Groups of ice houses become small cities in time.

They are no guarantees of success.

It's important that you learn to look for fish on your own. Sure, some well-known ice fishing spots produce every year. But many are good only at early ice, and only before the bigger, catchable fish have been taken, and hordes of footsteps and trucks and power augers pressure many of the remaining fish off the spot, or into non-aggressive feeding moods.

Even without fishing pressure, iced-over fisheries go through fairly distinct "seasons" or "periods." Roughly, you can divide them into (1) early ice, (2) midwinter, and (3) late ice.

Don't look for abrupt changes, but gradual transitions are noticeable. Stay with moving fish by keeping your eyes, and your options, open.

This chapter won't get into locational details on each species, but general tendencies can be just as important. Inevitably, it seems, no matter how much "detail" is provided on a given fish, a lot of things get missed or ignored. If you can tell all about finding bluegills in bigger natural lakes, you miss reservoirs, ponds and river backwaters. The best way to learn about the fish you seek, on the waters you frequent, is to use the tools at your disposal!

Early Ice

In general, wherever you find fish in late fall you find them at early ice. There is no mass movement, in other words, on the day ice forms.

Pre-ice scouting in a boat is probably the most universally-

Bluegills and other panfish are popular quarry for ice fishermen. This fisherman is staying very mobile as he successfully locates schools beneath the ice.

missed opportunity in fishing. Many people in the "ice belt" store their boats for winter, taking care of that task before hunting season.

If you can hold off putting the boat away, spend a few hours on several lakes you want to ice-fish. Look for concentrations of fish on your sonar. Where, exactly, you look will vary slightly with different species, but typical late fall (first ice) locations are:

• Shallow flats that hold baitfish and insects. They should be near deep water. Many have weeds on them in summer. Many have flooded timber and brush, or other cover. In general, the bigger and more complex (having different depth levels, "stair-step ledges," and a variety of cover) the better.

Key winter fish-holding locations on larger flats are depressions and are easy to find with a depthfinder (many show on lake maps). If weeds on the flat get matted down, fish use water depth as cover.

• Steep drop-offs, that lead from these shallow flats into the deeper water. Some fish, but not all, will hold along the drop-off itself.

• The base of steep drop-offs, and the deep "basin" water leading off of them. Often, fish will spend time sitting in the deep water, moving up onto the shallow flat to feed. Or, they may suspend in the basin area. When fish are "resting," they are not looking for a meal, but can often be coaxed with a precise presentation.

You'll see fish on your depthfinder in the deep water and along the drop-off. But don't expect to see many in shallow water; your "cone angle" is so narrow in water of 10 feet and less that not many big fish stick around to be detected in it.

(Of course, not all bodies of water have structure like these. In waters with little structure, look for points and humps, even if they don't rise significantly. Anything that roaming fish have to "go around" will concentrate some, giving you better odds of putting a lure in front of a few.)

• For some fish, especially panfish, relatively deep (say, 30-40 feet) bays or basins with soft bottom are the place to begin your search. Roam the basin with your sonar on, looking for groups of fish. Dave Genz of Minneapolis, Minnesota, who is fast becoming a legend in ice-fishing circles for his innovative methods and products, found a deep depression in a river backwater in the middle of summer, and thought it looked like a winter panfish spot. Using county road maps, he found a way to drive through the woods right to the bank. The first time he tried the spot after freeze-up it was suspicion confirmed: sunfish and crappies for supper!

At the very least, identify high-percentage structure to return to. Get shore markings so you can find them easily after the ice forms.

The first-ice bite, as many already know, can be very good on these shallow flats. But the fish are extremely spooky (normally, there's no snow to mask your movements). If you're after bigger fish like pike, bass and walleyes, tip-ups—because you can back away and watch them—are often a better bet than jigging over the top of fish.

Midwinter

It usually takes a month or so for the onset of what we call the midwinter period. Mostly, it has to do with oxygen levels. Heavy snow cover early—which cuts off light penetration and photosynthesis sooner—will accelerate the process, whereas years of less snow will slow it down.

At "early" midwinter, the first reaction of fish, generally speaking, is to spend more time in deeper water. The water is warmest, generally 39 degrees Fahrenheit, at the bottom of a frozen lake (and slightly above 32 just under the ice). As long as adequate oxygen holds out at the bottom of deep-water areas, they will hold lots of fish. But eventually, oxygen levels at the bottom can deteriorate also. (Bottom "ooze" eats oxygen.) It's common at this time of year to see fish begin to suspend more. In lakes with a lot of vegetation and mucky sediment, late-midwinter fish can be sort of "forced into the middle zone" of the water column. It could be a combination of environmental factors, that together leave the middle of the water column the best compromise zone of temperature and oxygen.

(Some experts also believe this fish suspension could be a plankton-driven phenomenon. Masses of plankton might, for example, "layer out" at certain levels of light intensity. That would draw baitfish and panfish, and in turn larger predators. You'll see concentrations of plankton on a good depthfinder,

Early winter's slick, open ice can be a time of fast action. It's best if you have done some scouting before ice-in, and a depthfinder set up to be portable can be a big help when it comes to locating fish.

and will notice that they move up and down in response to changing light conditions.)

Again, keep in mind that the timing and severity of the "oxygen problem" is regulated by the makeup of the body of water and the amount of snow cover. Generally speaking, deeper, less fertile lakes hold oxygen better than shallower, more fertile lakes; larger lakes hold oxygen better than smaller ones. A small, deep lake is not as likely to suffer "freeze-out" (where oxygen levels get low enough to kill large numbers of fish) as a small, shallow lake.

In general, fishing gets "deeper and tougher" as midwinter wears on. But by locating fish and working them with live bait presentations, using your depthfinder as a "mood indicator" (more on this in the next section) you can have better success

Finding Fish Under The Ice   129 now than most anglers do during the peak first-ice bite!

Late Ice

Finally, the weather warms enough to start melting the snow and top layer of ice. (Ice also melts from the bottom up, especially in shallow bays.) The still-frozen lakes get sloppy, with standing water all over. When you drill holes to fish, water runs down the hole and into the lake.

You're into the late ice period.

Soon, much of the standing water is gone. What happens is the ice breaks free from the bottom along shore and the whole ice pack, being lighter than water, "floats." You get open water, in fact, along dark-bottomed shoreline stretches.

You have to be careful and use common sense about your ice-fishing plans at this time of year. The ice gets rotten looking, or "honeycombs" as they say. You can often punch through 8 or 10 inches of ice with a 2x4.

Good clothing is important for enjoying ice fishing all winter, but it can save your life at late-ice. This includes Mustang's anti-exposure coveralls. They are comfortable and warm, and an ideal cold weather, open-water fishing outfit. It doubles as your personal flotation device while boating.

As long as the ice stays safe, the fishing gets good again. The action of the ice pack being lifted by rising water levels uproots frozen-in vegetation and insects. This can happen in any depth that supports standing weeds through the winter. (Frozen-in weeds have been seen as deep as 12 feet.) That, warming water, and increasing oxygen levels attract fish to shallow water zones again.

Many fish are staging near spawning areas, and the fishing can be excellent, where seasons are kept open. Keep catch-and-release in mind.

The Sonar Factor

It's amazing that many open-water anglers, who would feel lost without a depthfinder, go ice fishing without one.

You can either make or buy a holder for your sonar unit, that also holds a 12-volt motorcycle or gel-cell battery. A bracket holds the transducer in the water, and a leveling bubble keeps it shooting the signal straight down—this will be the key to seeing your lure at all times while checking fish activity.

Top ice anglers don't normally drill holes until they locate a likely spot and fish. They shoot their sonar signal through the ice (you can do this until the ice gets too thick and clouded with air bubbles, dirt, or whatever) and take as many readings as necessary to understand a piece of structure, find weed edges, or other cover, and see fish.

(Signals look exactly the same through the ice, or with the transducer in a drilled hole, as they do in summer. For more on general sonar use, see Chapter 5.)

Even on clean ice, you have to make a "seal" between the transducer and the ice surface to get a good reading. If the air temperature is above freezing, you can pour water on the ice. If it's colder than that, though, water will freeze to the bottom of the transducer and might ruin your sonar performance once it's set in the hole. In those conditions, mix windshield washer fluid with water in an empty dish-soap dispenser, and squeeze a little on the ice, setting the transducer in it.

(According to limnologists, because methyl alcohol evaporates well—and only minute amounts are poured on the ice—environmental impact of this practice is not a concern.)

Once you drill a hole to fish from, set the transducer in it. (When you hook a big fish, clear the transducer by pushing it out of the way with your foot.) A leveling bubble makes it easier to shoot the signal straight down.

Even a tiny ice jig will show up down to 30 feet or deeper, assuming your unit is of sufficient quality. Liquid crystals are passable ice fishing units, but flashers are far-and-away the best choice. Why? Their signals update quicker and more often, and that makes a real difference in performance. No matter how quickly you jiggle your bait, the flasher can keep up with your every move. If you move a bait quickly on a liquid crystal screen, its display will "trail" the movements.

That becomes important when a fish appears on your screen and you try to make it bite. A flasher shows everything. You jiggle, and you see the fish's reaction. Did it keep coming, or disappear from the screen? You experiment by slowly raising, and study the fish's reaction. Still won't bite? Try slowly lowering it. That did the trick!

The "trigger" changes from day to day, and even hour to

hour. With a flasher, you can change with it.

One flasher, the Vexilar FL8, shows tiny ice flies better than any other unit, and, its three-color display lets you watch as fish enter the edge of your cone (thin, green signals), come closer (thicker, yellow signals), and eventually directly under you (widening, brightening red). A unit like this is more expensive than other flashers, but worth every penny. You see your lure, and the fish. You see what the fish does in reaction to what you do. Heaven on earth!

The Principle Of Mobility

Think about it: do you sit in one spot all day when you're fishing from a boat or from shore? Of course not. If the fish don't bite, you keep moving.

And yet, the history of ice fishing is a case of arrested movement. Because of cold weather, the emphasis is put on comfort, not finding and catching fish. "Fish" houses are not fish houses at all if they can't be moved—even short distances—easily and at a moment's notice.

Now, another strong opinion. A fish house is not portable if it takes more than 30 seconds to set up, becomes difficult in the wind, and you have to do anything with your gloves off. If it has to be pulled behind a truck, has a heater running off a 20-pound propane tank, and if you brag about routinely fishing in a t-shirt on cold days, you are not mobile enough to be a consistently successful ice angler.

"Unless it's easy to move, you won't," says Genz, who, more than any single person, shined light on the silliness of our traditional ice-fishing methods.

Now, Genz and others market easily set up, portable ice houses that can be moved to a new location and set up again quickly so that you can be fishing in minutes. Things like 5-gallon buckets offer mobility. But it's nice to have a fish house that maintains its mobility while storing and protecting all the extra things you need (auger, delicate rods, depthfinder, lures and bait, heater, lunch, camera) for a day of fishing.

If you want a place to drink beer and play cards, go shopping for a nice 4x8-footer. Or perhaps an even larger house, with bunks, stove, refrigerator and television set.

Yes, I've heard the argument that in some regions it doesn't

This angler's efforts during a day on the ice was rewarded with a nice-sized perch. This fish was hugging the bottom in 23 feet of water.

get cold enough to require a shelter. But you need a way to haul your gear, including an auger. You can't hold it all in your hands, or in a 5-gallon bucket.

Besides, a portable shelter offers freedom from the wind. Even a breeze blows your line around, making it harder to detect bites. Walls and a ceiling also make it much easier to read a depthfinder display.

Whatever you use for a shelter and gear holder, the important thing is to stay mobile. Make it easy to move and you will. Keep moving, checking a variety of locations, and you'll eventually find fish. Then, it's up to you to catch them.

Tips For Catching Iced-Over Fish

It's not a bad idea to begin fishing with a vibrating "search" lure, to at least "call" fish into your hole. Examples include the Cicada, Sonar, Knocker Minnow and the Rattl'n Rapala.

If you get a lot of "follows" with these lures, try tipping them with maggots or even fish eyes (where legal) for more strike-triggering appeal.

Also, learn to "call" fish into your hole with a search lure, reel it up, and quickly drop a smaller, more subtle bait. That often results in an immediate bite.

Be constantly alert for suspended fish to pass into your sonar signal. Quickly reel up or let down to them.

Don't stay more than 10 or 15 minutes in one hole without a bite, unless you're on a known hotspot and believe strongly fish will move to you soon. However, if you've just driven up in your pickup and punched a hole with a power auger, you'll need to let the fish "settle down." Some anglers pre-drill holes and come back later to fish them. Also, if you catch a few quick fish in a hole and the bite slows—even if you still see fish on the sonar screen—move to a new hole. One of the only drawbacks to using sonar through the ice is that people get addicted to the "video game" of trying to make fish bite. Don't spend an hour trying to convert what Genz calls a "sniffer."

Realize that, while fish often bite readily during the prime hours of dusk and dawn, they can often be caught all day with the right approach. At midday, fish are not normally willing to move far to bite, so you have to put the bait right in front of them and tease them into striking. Live bait, and beyond that fresh live bait, is crucial. Don't try to see how many fish you can catch on the same maggot, or minnow.

Fish Finding
Lures

=11=

The Versatile Jig

ere's what a television commercial comparing old jigging methods to new might look like. It could open with a black-and-white sequence of a boat anchored or slowly drifting over a "deep hole," serene string music playing while the occupants, an older couple, patiently wait for a strike.

Cut to heavy metal rock-and-roll, full living color, and guide and tournament pro Daryl Christensen holding position in heavy waves with a bow-mounted trolling motor. He's slicing cast after cast into prime shallow structure, covering it fast and thoroughly. It's aggressive.

Jump cut to Dick "The Griz" Grzywinski, a well-known guide. He's forward-trolling at a good clip, whipping his rodtip to keep his lure hopping. It's called "Rip Jigging" and by using it, he catches more fish in a day than most people would catch in a summer.

Slowly dissolve back to the old boat, still in the same place. Still waiting. You have to lean into the television to see if they're still breathing. "The fish will be here any minute now, Martha ..." The commercial comes to an end with a flurry of two quick freeze frames, one of Christensen with a huge walleye and the other one with "The Griz" struggling to hold up a 7-pound largemouth bass.

Often hailed as the universal antidote to fishless days, the leadhead jig is the essence of simplicity. Hook and sinker in

Jigs are a popular lure for walleyes as evidenced by this big walleye that fell victim to a jig.

The Versatile Jig

one. The one lure to carry in your survival kit, they say.

But what a transformation it has undergone!

Not just in design, which has been impressive enough; but in application. Today's jigging methods imitate yesterday's like today's fast-breaking, slam-dunking NBA basketball resembles two-handed set shots into bushel baskets.

To put it bluntly, jigs are not thought of as "water-covering" lures. The jig is, indeed, versatile. But it's like the proverbial puppet on a string. It can't do anything without you. It's not so much the jig that's versatile as the man, woman or child behind the rod and reel. You add the music, and move the jig as slow or fast as you prefer.

"People can't believe how fast I fish with a jig," says Christensen, "or how many fish I catch on them. But I always ask them to watch carefully, and compare how fast I fish a jig to how fast they fish a crankbait. I'm still moving slower than most of them are with a crankbait. Jigs don't have to be crawled along the bottom, you know."

He laughs that laugh of the guide.

The Possibilities

We already know that jigs are good for slowly probing known fish hideouts. They'll always be good for that, and in some situations (examples: after cold fronts, and during periods of extremely cold water, like spring and fall) it's probably the best way to fish a jig. The goal here is to point out the possibilities.

Think of it as an old lure—jigs—applied to a relatively new idea: covering water quickly, looking for active fish.

If your eyes start to water, you can always slow down.

Christensen on speed-jigging by casting: "People would catch a lot more fish on jigs if they'd just use them more. You need to open your eyes to the different situations where they're a good choice.

"For example, let's talk about shallow fish. The reason people don't catch shallow fish is they spook them before they put a bait in front of them. You need to assume fish are in good-looking shallow spots, like bays with shoreline cover, or reefs that top off shallow. Don't go cruising over the spot looking to see if fish are there. They're gone if you try that.

While jigs are not thought of as "water-covering" lures, guide and tournament pro Daryl Christensen has developed a method of using jigs in quickly casting shallow-water areas. This method can help you locate and catch more fish.

"Stay back and cast a light jig. Try using 6-pound line instead of what you normally use. It'll cast farther. (Some anglers go as light as 4-pound test when using ⅟₁₆-ounce jigs.) Shallow fish are scattered fish, and they're feeding fish. They're looking for something to eat. They're active and aggressive, so you don't have to give them an ultra-slow presentation."

Examples of good shallow-water jigs include Bait Rigs' Slo-Poke and Walleye Willospoon, and the Swimmin' Fuzz-E-Grub from Lindy Tackle. The Willospoon is an extremely light jig that should be fished under a float if you're trying to cast it any distance.

Wind Jigging

"If you get a good wind, you can really fish a jig,"

Christensen says. "Most guys quit jig-fishing when the wind blows. I want wind. I like a minimum of 3-footer waves." (Daryl is an experienced boater running an 18-foot, seaworthy craft. As always, fish in winds only until they become too unruly for your boat and your boating skills.)

"Get fairly close to the spot. Wind hides you, so you can get fairly close to the fish. Position yourself so you can cast parallel to the wind and let your jig just wash away from you at an angle, right in the wave trough. It's almost like fishing river current. If you were to cast it straight downwind and leave your bail open, the wind would carry the jig straight away from you. But you're casting it out sort of parallel to the wind, and jigging it in at the same time as it's being washed away from you. So the jig is sort of going away and coming toward you at the same time, if that makes sense.

"It's so simple it's just ridiculous. You cast into the wave trough and let the jig go for a ride. There's nothing to it," Christensen explains.

"And the thing is, you can cast a long ways and then you don't really have to do anything, because those wave troughs will take a ⅛- or ¹⁄₁₆-ounce jig with a leech or piece of nightcrawler and swim it all over the place. All I do is keep my line tight."

Depending on the wind, he says, you might need to help the jig along so it doesn't hang up on bottom. It just takes a touch, a skill many anglers have never developed because they haven't tried this method. Christensen believes strongly that, when fished as a searching lure, jigs should not usually be contacting bottom.

"I try to keep it from going on the bottom," he says. "When most fish hit that thing in those waves, I mean they really slam it. And some people say they can't feel the bite when it's windy. You don't have to feel it, but you better hang on to your rod."

Christensen chooses either a ¹⁄₁₆- or ⅛-ounce jig partly based on how fast he wants to fish. If he's trying to cover water quickly, he'll go to the ⅛-ouncer or even a ¼-ouncer, reeling fast and trying to draw strikes from active fish. If the fish are proving to be sluggish or finicky, he'll probably drop down to the ¹⁄₁₆-ouncer, which offers a slower presentation.

Christensen feels that "wind jigging" is superior to slip-

Wind Jigging

In "wind jigging," cast into a wave trough, roughly parallel to the wind, and let the natural "current" wash your jig down and away from you. Let it ride through the area you want to cover, putting only enough tension on to keep it off the bottom.

bobbering on spots that have vastly uneven bottom contours. By feeling for your jig to tick bottom and then raising it off, you can cover wildly changing depths, down to maybe 10 feet, depending on jig weight and wave strength.

An important point: Virtually all search-fishing with jigs is done in water less than 15 feet deep. Beyond that, the jig is not an efficient tool; it can't be fished quickly enough.

Speed-Jigging By Trolling

Dick Grzywinski knows about speed-jigging by trolling. "The Griz" is a regionally famous St. Paul, Minnesota, guide known for keeping customers on the water long after sunburn sets in.

He's a top-flight angler who knows that fish aren't in the

Spend a day on the water with Dick "The Griz" Grzywinski and you'll earn your hat! Spend some time learning the finer points of Dick's "rip jigging" technique, and you'll be catching more fish on your own.

same spot every day. He likes the search, and has a jigging method that really covers water fast. It's a wrinkle that will work for you. He calls it "rip jigging."

Before attempting it, read about it carefully. Even before that, wipe your mind's slate clean of everything you know about jig fishing. Forget every rule about presentation and boat control you've ever heard.

In short, what Griz does is troll forward along contours, weed edges or other likely areas. He casts a jig out as he's moving, a lot closer to the boat than you might think ("to heck with the thought that fish will spook from the boat").

Then, he settles in for a long day of snapping his wrist. Aggressively, he works his jig, a special homemade feather-duster he makes himself. You can quickly look over long shoreline breaks, large reefs and points and other large areas. Or, you can make a pass over a good spot, wheel around and come back through it. It's a great way to fish while you try to learn a new body of water.

It sounds simple, and it is. But like all simple, effective systems, there are small details that spell the difference between success and failure.

"The main thing," Griz says, "is to go out and do it, and experiment with getting the boat to move right. Boat control is very important."

Moving the boat right means:

● Motoring into the wind or current. This lets you control your movements easier, and lessens the chance of moving too fast. Because he always moves forward, Griz doesn't have

Motoring Into The Wind

WIND ⟶

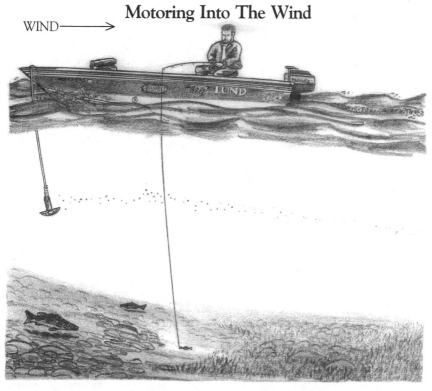

First, motor forward into the wind. Cast out a ¼- or ⅛-ounce jig, tipped with a minnow hooked through the eyes. While Dick Grzywinski fishes the jig quite close to the boat, you can drop back 30 to 40 feet if you're worried about spooking fish.

The Versatile Jig

"splash guards" installed on his boat, a standard on most North-country rigs. He is comfortable in heavy seas that send many backtrollers to shore. To stabilize his movements in rough water, he tosses out a sea anchor that's tied on a short rope to the bow eye. "It keeps you moving straight, just like you're tied to a dock." (The short rope is critical, or the sea anchor could twist up in your motor.)

• Putting the boat over the precise depth that's holding the fish you want to catch. Fish often hold at definite depth zones, which change from season to season and day to day. Once you catch a few fish at a certain depth, keep on that depth. On some days, deviating as little as 6 inches or a foot can mean no more bites, Griz maintains!

• Also, train yourself to notice the little things, like isolated hard-bottom areas in expanses of soft bottom, edges of weeds, the crest of a rock reef or sand point. Griz is practically world famous for catching tons of fish among other boats that are only picking up stragglers. "A lot of times," he says, "they don't realize that they're only a few feet from all the fish."

How heavy is the jig? He prefers a ¼-ounce feathered "Griz Jig" or Northland Fireball. But, he will use ⅛-ouncers in shallower water or when he wants to slow things down a bit.

How far should you cast out? Griz keeps the lure amazingly close. "In deeper water," he says, "you gotta be farther behind the boat. (He uses the method in water as deep as 25 feet, but average anglers would probably do best at 15 feet or less, especially while learning it.) It depends a lot on whether the water is clear or cloudy. In dirty water, or on real windy days, you can troll right over the fish and they'll still bite. But I'd say that most of the time I'm not more than 25 or 30 feet behind the boat. The jig drags on the bottom if you cast too far out."

(Try the rule of more line for clear and/or deep water; less for dirty and shallow, even if it seems that shallow fish would be spooky and would require a longer-distance approach. Griz invented the method and wrote the rule book, and it works for him so it should work for you, too.)

How do you know how deep your jig is running?

Griz goes by 35 years of accumulated feel. With as much time as he spends on the water, that's like 245 dog years to you and me.

Mortals will have to experiment. Griz does not try to bounce the jig off bottom to know where it is, but you might try that for awhile. Speed up a touch and assume you're just off. When the jig hits weeds, rip it again and it normally comes free. You can work this method through thick weeds and other cover that would stop slip-sinker rigs and crankbaits.

Should you tip it with live bait?

Griz likes fathead minnows. Any smallish, tough minnow should work well. Hook it through both eyeballs and it stays on the hook fairly well through the rigors of ripping.

How heavy should the line be?

Griz has settled mainly on 10-pound-test monofilament. "I'm ripping the jig so hard that I tear the line and break it all the time with 8-pound. I don't have any problems with 12-pound, but I like using 10-pound better. Still, I have to re-tie about every hour or even the 10-pound snaps off."

What kind of a jigging motion is it?

As for the "rip" or the snap itself . . . you guessed it . . . it's all in the wrist.

"Get comfortable," Griz says. "I like to put my right leg up on my tackle box and get settled in. It's all wrist action. Don't use your arm or it drags the jig too much. You want that thing hopping around back there.

"Hold your rodtip down toward the water, and make a strong snap with your wrist, maybe about 3 feet forward. Don't raise your rodtip or it'll lift the jig too high. Snap your rod really quick forward, and follow the line back slowly so you can feel a hit."

Don't keep the line tight while you follow it back, or the jig won't sink and do its stuff. And, take heart if you're worried about being able to feel subtle strikes: You often hook the fish when you go to make the next wrist-snap! Instant hookset. It even happens to Griz sometimes.

It will feel strange to fish so close to the boat. (Through the years, Griz has found, especially in cloudier water, that he's able to fish as close as 8 feet behind the boat and catch fish in as shallow as 6 feet of water without spooking problems!)

Go farther back, especially in deeper and clearer water. But take in line or speed up if you're dragging bottom. Above all, when you first try this, ignore the little voices of reason in the

Sophisticated European-influenced floats can be perfect partners for jigs, especially if you're searching shallow water and want to cast from a distance but slowly work the jig through prime areas. From left are the Thill Mini Stealth, Ice'n Fly Special, Stream'n Brook Master; and the Wille snap-on float.

back of your head. Because once you get the hang of "rip jigging," your smile may have to be surgically removed.

Fishing Jigs Under Slip Floats

Especially when you want to use ultra-light jigs (say, anything ¹⁄₁₆ ounce and lighter), a float can be a big help.

Floats can help increase casting distance of extremely light jigs, and suspend them at a pre-determined depth. You can quickly move the jig-and-float combo into a good-looking spot, then let it sit, tempting even negative fish (those that are not likely to bite).

Jig-and-float rigs are often used by spring panfish anglers, who want to let a light jig wash with the waves, or who cover water by reeling in under calm conditions.

If you're working very shallow water for spooky fish, use a small float that doesn't make a big splash. Thill Tackle's Mini Stealth or Ice'n Fly Special are ideal for still water. The Stream'n Brook Master works beautifully in river current.

Class Tackle also makes a line of sophisticated floats that match well with light jigs. And Wille has a snap-on slip float that goes on your line without having to re-tie.

These European-influenced floats are much more stream-lined and functional than traditional American products. With the slightest pull, a properly-balanced float signals the bite.

Summing Up

Jigs can be used at virtually any depth. But for covering water quickly, they are probably only efficient down to approximately 15 feet.

To quickly put a bait past fish below 15 feet, you're better off running something like a crankbait, spinner rig or even a live bait on a plain hook, behind a bottom bouncer. Then, if you can't get a bite, it might be time to slowly work over those fish with a vertical jigging presentation.

You can always slow down. Just remember to speed up, in the right situations, and jigs become as versatile as advertised.

=12=

Fishing With Lures

E ven old hands at the fishing game sometimes become frustrated in selecting from the myriad of artificial lures on the market because new types are being offered every day. There are crankbaits, minnow imitators, chuggers, darters, divers, flashers, plunkers, poppers, rattlers, splashers, splutters, swimmers and wobblers, in many sizes and in numerous color combinations for fishing on the surface, for floating and diving, for deep running for bottom bumping and much more.

How do you make a reasonable selection that will tempt fish to strike under most circumstances? First, you need to understand that these baits fall into two basic categories: those fished on or near the surface and those fished beneath the surface. It's a good idea to have three or four of each type of lure in your tackle box in sizes or weights to suit the type of fish you're after, but you can easily get by with fewer. These, wisely chosen, will suit most conditions and will provide the varied actions or sounds that tempt fish to strike.

Color combinations are also perplexing in their infinite variety. They are much less important than type. Start with only one color combination (say silver and black) of each type in the middle range (as discussed in Chapter 2). Later on, it will be helpful to own darker and lighter ones.

From there, novice fishermen can broaden their collection as their fishing horizons expand. Added color combinations

When you're outfitting your tackle box, don't overlook plastic worms for inclusion among lures that take fish. This bass was quite happy to go for this plastic worm presentation.

Fishing With Lures

may take to your eye, and there are other types you may want to try, as well as newer innovations, some of which should be regarded with suspicion. But depend on the old standbys which have been on the market for years because they have proved themselves.

Floating-Diving Baits

Floating-diving baits lie on the surface at rest, but submerge on the retrieve. When line tension is released, they pop back to the surface again. The action is produced by a metal or plastic lip. The depth that the lure dives depends on the size and cant of the lip. Minnow-imitations have already been discussed so they won't be covered here. Crankbaits, vibrating baits and trolling lures will be covered.

Crankbaits are not new, they have been catching fish for years, but several specialty lures have come out in recent months. A crankbait is any lure with a plastic or metal tip that causes it to dive and move when retrieved or trolled. Generally, you can judge how deep a crankbait will go by the size and shape of its lip. A short, steep-sloping lip will run shallow, while a bait with a long, straight lip will run deeper.

Crankbaits are fished in two ways: casting and trolling. Casting is by far the most popular method for bass fishermen who often concentrate their efforts in shallow water. The basic retrieve is simply to reel at a medium to rapid rate, but it pays to vary your retrieve until you find what works best. As a general rule, slow retrieves work best in cold water and faster retrieves work better in warm.

Vibrating baits, like crankbaits, dive upon retrieve, but they lack the diving lip. The position of the eye makes them dive and vibrate when retrieved. The vibrations are intensified by a sound chamber that causes a rattle as the lure swims. Some vibrating baits have several eye positions to allow a selection of hook-ups for near-surface or deep fishing, but most have only one. Select one or two in colors similar to prevalent baitfish, and perhaps a lighter and darker one for different water and weather conditions.

The last lure category to be discussed is trolling baits. These lures, while similar to crankbaits, share one common feature: They're difficult to cast. The J-plug, for example, is designed to

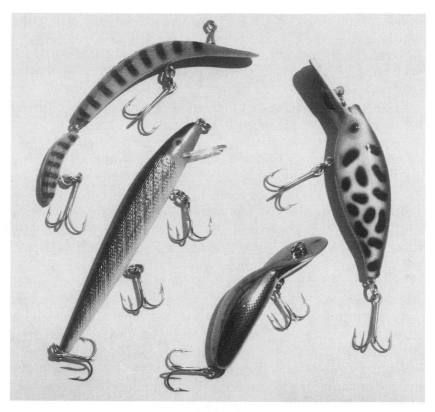

Plugs come in many different forms including (clockwise from bottom) the Lunker Licker crankbait, the Minnow Float and trolling plugs—FlatFish and Tadpolly. Most plugs come equipped with treble hooks.

float up the line when a fish is hooked. Others, like the Believer, are simply too heavy to cast all day. There is a wide variety of trolling plugs available, and they will take everything from salmon and steelhead to muskies, walleyes and bass. When selecting lures, consider the species you are fishing and the depth you are running.

Surface Lures

Surface lures are designed to look edible to fish even when lightly cast and allowed to sit on the water until the ripples have subsided. A fish may rise and smack the floater as soon as it alights. If this doesn't happen in productive water, you can be pretty sure fish are eyeing the offering and trying to make up their minds whether they want it for dinner. A slight twitch, followed by a pause and a few more twitches, may tempt the fish. Keep the line tight and under control. From then on, fish the lure in a variety of manners until you find the most productive. All lures are fished with different actions and at different speeds.

The propbait is typical of lures with propellers either at head or tail or both. The revolving blades make it splutter in motion, so it works best on a fairly calm surface. After the cast-pause-twitch method just described, pull it through the water just fast enough to make the blades revolve, stopping it every few feet. Fish may strike when it moves slowly. If not, speed up the retrieve gradually. A rule is to work baits faster in warmer water because fish are more active then, and slower in colder water for the opposite reason. Another rule is to start slowly and to gradually speed up the action until you get strikes.

The crawler family of surface lures, which includes the Jitterbug as its most famous member, has been with us for many years. Crawler-type lures are well-known for their excellent action. Their cupped metal lip or hinged wing pushes the surface water, causing the lure to wobble from side to side with a plopping sound. The baits work best with a moderately fast retrieve making them good for covering lots of water fast. They're also excellent for night fishing.

Another bait with a very different action is the minnow-imitation. The original Rapala now has many counterparts, such as the Rebel, A.C. Shiner, Bagley Bang-O-Lure, Bomber Long A and others. Most minnow-imitations float, but some sink. The majority of minnow-imitations run fairly shallow, say 1 to 6 feet, but many of the newer models will run up to 20 feet deep or more.

A variety of ways exist to fish minnow-type lures, from twitching them on the surface for bass, to trolling them deep for walleyes or salmon. Tailor the methods and lures you fish to the species you are pursuing.

Tackle stores offer many varieties of poppers or chuggers in all shapes, sizes and colors. The Hula Popper is probably the best known, followed by the Lucky 13. Poppers are easy to fish. Simply cast them near shoreline cover and retrieve them with short, sharp twitches of the rodtip. The lure will jump and push water ahead of it because of its concave head, thus making a slight pop. This adds the enticement of sound.

I like the Hula Popper because the plastic skirt fluffs on each pop to provide added motion, and because the skirt can be quickly changed to one of another color. Other types of poppers are dressed with tails of hair, feathers and synthetic materials. Some have small wobbling spoons as tails.

Stickbaits, like the famous Zaro Spook, are known for their effectiveness on a variety of fish. They are fished in a "walk-the-dog" fashion where the back of the lure swings from side to side when retrieved with short, sharp jerks. Light line is best because it doesn't impede the lure's action.

The jerkbait is also an excellent surface lure, especially for muskies and giant northern pike. A jerkbait is fished on heavy equipment. A stiff rod with a long handle will help you do so properly. After casting, retrieve the jerkbait in sharp sweeps of the rod. Remember to reel the slack in quickly so you can set the hook effectively.

In selecting any of these lures, it is better to try the smallest ones that suit the tackle. Big fish will take small lures, but small fish have trouble with big ones.

Many fishermen are content with surface lures and want nothing else because they enjoy the thrill of seeing smashing strikes on top. Good surface fishing usually occurs only at certain times of day and at certain seasons. At least 90 percent of the time we find fish deep.

=13=

Fooling Fish With Spinners

Spinners for casting or trolling attract gamefish by flash and sound. Fishermen often buy and use them haphazardly, not realizing that they must be selected and fished properly.

Among the many and varied types of blades used for spinners, a few stand out. All are attractors whose whirling glint seems to simulate the flash of baitfish. In addition, they emit throbbing sound, perhaps imperceptible to humans, but so clearly heard by fish that they seek and strike at it even in discolored water where the spinners can't be seen clearly. The throbbing effect seems most pronounced in spinners which revolve at the greatest angle to the lure's shaft.

Next in importance in throbbing effect is the thin Colorado blade when it is used as a spinner. Many lures are marketed with this type of blade. Their egg-shaped, concave blade is rigged to revolve at nearly 45 degrees from the shaft to provide moderate sound pulsations and considerable flash. It's a proven fish-catcher.

The well-known Indiana blade is also thin and concave, but a little longer. It spins at an angle of only about 15 degrees from the shaft, producing faint sound pulsations but considerable flash. These light, concave blades spin actively under minimum pull or current pressure.

The willowleaf blade is long, narrow and pointed, just like a willow leaf, hence its name. It spins close to the shank,

This bass went after a spinner with a vengeance, probably because he considered it a noisy intruder that had to be attacked.

providing minimum sound pulsations, but considerable flash. It is a clear-water blade whose long shape and narrow spin most accurately simulates the appearance of baitfish.

Three others are notable here. The propeller blade rotates on a shaft through its center and thus is one of the noisiest ones. For this reason, it is popular on plugs because it provides sound, flash and splash. These blades provide average pulsations and considerable flash.

Shapes, weights and curvatures present problems in physics that don't need to be bothered with here. The important point is to use blades that provide the desired amount of noise or throb coupled with the amount of flash that is needed to attract fish under various water conditions.

Colors of blades are less important. Silver may be preferable for dull days and deep or murky water and brass or copper for brighter conditions, but this also depends on the amount of flash they provide. A bright blade reflecting sunlight can be so bright that it will repel fish rather than attract them. Some blades are partially black for this reason. Other colors may be mainly for identification or decoration. It does no harm to let blades tarnish. You may want them that way on sunny days. They can be polished quickly with a piece of crocus cloth if needed.

How To Fish Spinners

In lake fishing, an erratic retrieve usually works better than a steady one. Cast and let the spinner sink on just enough loose line so it will drop to the level where the fish should be. Fish it in with a few cranks of the reel handle, let it flutter down and repeat. Or raise the rod 2 or 3 feet, drop it back to let the spinner settle, and quickly regain slack line.

In stream fishing in shallow water, the rodtip should be kept high to keep the spinner off bottom. In deeper water, best results are obtained by casting quartering upstream and across. Let the spinner sink to the desired level. Then keep the blade throbbing while the current carries the lure downstream. Always plan casts, or the travel of the spinner, to direct it to good holding positions. In mild current, you may do better to cast cross-stream or quartering downstream. When fish are not showing, the object is to work the lure so it just ticks bottom.

Spinning lures are excellent for discolored water, especially during or after a rain when fish are on the feed. Remember the value of tiny spinning lures with fly rods or ultra-light spinning tackle. When strikes are few, it often helps to "sweeten" the hook with a worm, a light, slim pork-rind strip or some other artificial flutterer such as a pennant cut from balloon rubber.

These Marvelous Spinnerbaits

Few anglers fail to appreciate spinnerbaits because anyone who has ever used one probably caught fish. They are deadly for bass, pike, crappies and walleyes, and even trout are caught on them occasionally. Some anglers say that spinnerbaits are second only to the properly fished plastic worm, for catching more fish. I say these people are too easily forgetting about crankbaits, but I do share their enthusiasm for this wonderful lure. They are almost completely weedless, and work through heavy weeds or brush without snagging.

Spinnerbaits can be fished deep or on the surface. For surface fishing, the retrieve is started immediately so the spinner blade (or blades) flop along with a flashing, wriggling motion. An alternative is to retrieve the bait just under the surface, or a bit farther down. Let it sink a bit, reel it steadily for a few feet, let it sink again, and keep repeating the action. It is wise to experiment between steady retrieves and the retrieve-and-pause method to see what works best on the body of water you are fishing.

These lures can be worked up or down drop-offs in the manner one would fish a jig. Cast to the thin water of a drop-off, let the lure settle, raise the rod 2 or 3 feet to pull the lure off the incline, let it settle again, and so forth. When fishing up a drop-off, cast out as far as possible and give the lure time to settle. When it touches bottom, raise the rodtip about 3 feet just fast enough to feel the spinners turning. Drop the rodtip while reeling in slack, and keep repeating.

When fishing along bottom, let the lure sink as far as desired, pull it up and in as just described, and repeat several times. Then start a slow, deep retrieve just fast enough to be sure the spinners are turning.

A good choice for bottom-hugging fish such as walleyes is the weight-forward spinners. The fast-sinking design also is good for smallmouth, trout and northern pike, as well. Since they can be cast a long distance, they also work for reaching surface schools of white and striped bass.

A lead body sits ahead of the spinner and either a single or treble hook. A bob cast works better than a snap cast as the lure tends to tangle easily. However, the lure will not twist the line so the line should be attached directly to the lure, rather than to a swivel snap.

Weight-forward spinners work well with the "countdown" technique and will help maintain a relatively constant depth on the retrieve.

14

Spoons

Think back to the roots of your fishing life. A kid with a dull green tackle box from the hardware store. A river, stream, small lake, pond. It doesn't matter. You're excited and ready to go.

You're by yourself, or with your best friend. Nobody to teach you, so you both tie on spoons and start casting out there. The first jolting strike hooks you as deeply as the fish.

Later, you start learning more. Perhaps a parent or uncle takes you in a boat, shows you a few of the ropes. Next thing you know you're much too sophisticated to be seen fishing with a common spoon.

Why does this happen? Some of the most famous lures of all time are spoons. Hallowed names like Daredevle, Sutton, Doctor, and Red Eye Wiggler. The deadly fish-catching wobble and simplicity of spoons appeal universally to a wide variety of gamefish. When it comes to searching for fish, to versatility of casting and trolling, shallow or deep, spoons might be the all-time champions.

So why do they get shunned by so many "sophisticated," knowledgeable anglers?

Very good question.

Spoons are terrific at everything they do. Specialized types cover a vast array of conditions. If you've lost touch with spoons, maybe it's time for a reunion. Don't be afraid to buy a selection and put them to use.

The dedicated spoon fisherman will recognize these old standbys which when arranged on an old, beat-up tackle box says eloquently that a fisherman hangs onto what works.

Overall Spoon Basics

Similar to crankbaits, each spoon has a speed at which its wobble is most pronounced. You need to experiment to find it, by trolling each spoon at boatside or making a short cast and retrieving where you can see it.

(The most pronounced wobble is not always what the fish want, so you should try different spoons with tighter or wider wobbles until you find a preference. Also, by fishing a wide-wobbling spoon slower or faster than its "optimum" speed, you can get different actions.)

Spoons are often thought of as primarily "vision" lures; that is, fish strike them because they can see them. But the vibration patterns given off by a spoon are also picked up by the fish's lateral line. So don't entirely write them off in dirtier water.

They represent wounded, crippled or panicked baitfish. Those are signals predator fish understand, loud and clear.

Casting With Spoons

Casting to cover water quickly is perhaps where spoons shine most brightly.

"Chunking" as they call it in some parts, can be as scientific or haphazard as you like. But try to think about what you want to accomplish, rather than just randomly throwing casts.

First, carefully consider the size and type of spoon you want to use. You'll notice that different shaped spoons have fairly different actions. The same is true for spoons that are relatively thick or thin.

Thicker, heavier spoons cast farther and sink faster than thinner versions. If you're working shallow water, don't pick a thick, heavy spoon. Common sense.

Put each successive cast in a different location as you cover a spot, but don't hesitate to plunk several into a particularly good-looking area, such as the outside edge of a weedline or the base of a thick stump. Vary your retrieve if you lay down more than one cast in the same spot. Try a steady pull one time and a staggering, stop-and-go the next.

(This might sound obvious, but many anglers don't pay attention to where they have and haven't cast. Don't make work out of it, but keep track.)

Try not to splash the lure on top of a prime target. Rather, cast beyond it and work the lure into the holding spot. A spoon crashing down on top of even a big fish can scare it into the next county.

Weedless spoons, such as Johnson's famous Silver Minnow, are excellent for quickly running over thick cover. You can often draw a slashing strike from a fish holding in weeds or "wood." If you don't hook the fish, reel in quickly and fire another cast just beyond the same spot with a lure that can be fished slowly, such as a Texas-rigged plastic worm. (Yes, you should have at least two rods, at the ready, at all times.) It's amazing how many follow-up strikes you get when you float that worm through the same location.

Wear good polarizing sunglasses, and look for lanes and pockets in weeds or brush/stump concentrations. Quickly pull the weedless spoon over the most tangle-filled areas, then stop reeling to let it flutter down into the pockets. Work it deep through the open lanes. If you just cast and reel, cast and reel, you won't catch many fish unless they're committing suicide, as they say.

Continually experiment with retrieve speed and style. Make

Casting To Prime Targets

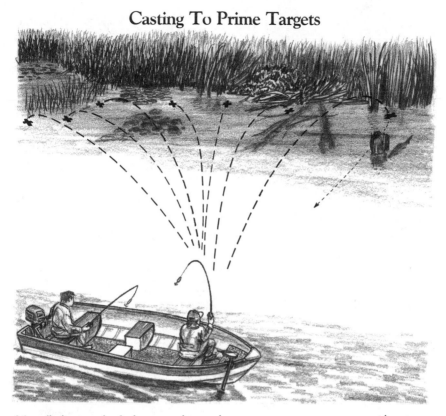

Mentally keep track of where you place each cast as you try to cover water with a spoon. And, be sure to cast well beyond a prime shallow-water target and then work it into the area so you don't spook fish holding there.

a note of what you were doing when each fish strikes. Some days they want a fast-moving bait that's trying to get away; other days, they aren't willing to chase. Figure out the pattern and you can have a memorable day.

Small spoons that cast well but don't create a belly-flop when they hit the water can be deadly tools for reaching out to shallow, spooky fish. Tournament pro Mike McClelland showed me a tactic he uses to fish walleyes in as little as 1 or 2 feet of water, by keeping his boat out deeper and bombing in long casts with a little silvery spoon. When it hits the water, he dances it like a crippled minnow, and the fish often respond. It would work on other species, too.

Spoons are like jigs, in that much of their action and effectiveness depend on you. Choose a spoon that casts as far as you need to at the moment, in a size and color appropriate for the fish you're after. Then, toss out all the rules. Try different things until something works.

Then, you will have written a chapter on how to catch fish using spoons.

Trolling With Spoons

For a lot of reasons, spoons are a natural choice for trolling. The wobbling action often doesn't need much enhancement. They hook fish well, and they don't dig down on their own when used behind downrigger balls or other heavy weights such as bottom bouncers.

Trolling, after all, was invented for covering water quickly in search of active fish.

Again, choose a spoon that fits what you want to do. Many are made with trolling in mind—thin, wispy bodies that dance at the slightest pull. Spoons that are too light to cast often make the best trolling partners.

When searching for fish in vast open spaces (a frontier being explored more and more), anglers often get fooled by seeing fish on their sonar units in fairly deep water. Rarely do fish display shallower than about 10 feet.

That doesn't mean fish aren't shallow. Big, feeding fish are often within 10 feet of the surface in very deep water. That's why one of the cardinal rules of basin trolling, as taught by Gary Parsons and Keith Kavajecz, is to put out at least one line that runs in about 5 feet or less. (Fish often come up to hit trolled lures, but rarely down.)

This lure can be either flatlined (run straight behind the boat, not hooked to a planer board or outrigger), or set out to the side using a planer board or ski. If you flatline it, make sure to let out lots of line, about 100 feet or so. Shallow fish scatter when the boat approaches (the reason they don't normally show up on sonar), and you have to give them time to settle before the lure gets to them.

You don't need to let out as much line if you hook up a planer board. Small boards like the Wille Side-Liner work beautifully.

Spoons, as mentioned, also work wonderfully behind downrigger balls. Set the ball depth and you know the lure

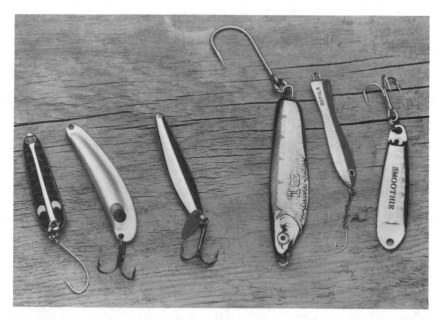

Heavy jigging spoons designed primarily for vertical fishing include (from left) the Hawger Spoon and Knocker Minnow, Swedish Pimple, Crippled Herring, Pilkki and Hopkins.

depth, although some lighter spoons do tend to rise a bit from water resistance. But at least you know approximately how deep your lure is running.

What About Jigging Spoons?

At first glance, jigging spoons might not seem to fit the concept of "exploratory" fishing. After all, they are mainly a "vertical" lure, right?

And when searching for fish, you don't want to slow down enough to fish a vertical lure, right?

But there are classes of jigging spoons, some more aggressive than others. The heavier, faster-falling models can be fairly good for quickly probing deeper water; and more streamline versions are made for swimming presentations, ala Daryl Christensen's "speed jigging."

Realize that crankbaits are probably better for covering vast amounts of territory. Think about pulling out the jigging spoons when you're in known fish-holding turf, but need to move constantly to stay with them.

Here are examples of heavy jigging spoons designed

Other jigging spoons glide well when worked "horizontally," making them good for swimming presentations. Examples include the Wing Wally (left) and Walleye Hawger (right).

primarily for vertical fishing:

The Hawger Spoon and Knocker Minnow, which has rattles; the Swedish Pimple; the Crippled Herring; the Pilkki; and the Hopkins. There are numerous others, but these are all good examples.

Now, some that work well for swimming presentations:

The Wing Wally and the Walleye Hawger. Again, there are many others.

Jigging spoons work, says Kavajecz, because they offer a "different look" to the fish than many traditional jigging lures. "They flutter and give off flash points," he says, "and a lot of times, it's enough to trigger bites from otherwise reluctant fish."

When fishing jigging spoons quickly, work them in long sweeping motions. Let the spoon fall back after pulling it forward on controlled slack line.

Casey Clark, a schoolteacher from Michigan, uses virtually nothing but Hopkins spoons, regardless of what kind of fish he's after. He catches a lot of fish. He has won tournaments, in fact, on spoons.

He says you need to let a spoon flutter somewhat freely for it to work its magic, but don't get sloppy with the slack or you won't feel the bites. It might be another new skill for you to work on, this business of sweeping a spoon forward, then "catching it softly," feeling all the while for a telltale tick.

But isn't learning new tricks what fishing is all about?

15

Fly Rod Artificials

Much of what has been written about fly fishing gives the impression that catching fish on artificial flies is a complicated art requiring years of practice, abnormal skill, expensive equipment and vast knowledge. Let's correct that impression by saying that anyone with passable equipment who can cast 30 feet can catch fish on artificials. Thirty feet isn't very far, and more fish are caught inside this range than outside it. You don't need many flies as long as you have a variety of sizes. All that's needed to get strikes is to drift wet or dry flies over good holding positions. You won't hook as many big ones as the experts do, but you'll catch fish and have fun.

Streamers And Bucktails

Gamefish take these long flies because they think they are baitfish, but also out of anger, curiosity or in the spirit of play. To learn how to fish them, lie on a dock and watch baitfish as they dart about, turning and grubbing along the bottom to show their shimmering sides while searching for food. Note their actions, their colors and their shapes. Try to imitate these when you are fishing.

While doing this, you should quickly come to the conclusion that most streamers and bucktails purchased commercially are overdressed, pleasing anglers more than the fish. This is not to say that correctly dressed old standbys such as the

Dry and wet flies, weighted streamers and bucktails are all part of the array of lures that the successful trout angler keeps at hand for different and changing conditions.

Gray Ghost, the Supervisor and the Black Ghost, for example, aren't as effective as they always were. It is to say that slimmer patterns on many occasions may be better. There are exceptions. The Muddler Minnow, which simulates a little bottom-feeder called the sculpin, is a fat fly which also is taken as a nymph or, when floating, as a grasshopper. Few minnow imitations are as versatile as this.

These flies should also be about the same size as prevalent baitfish, but since schools may include baitfish of various sizes, this isn't of major importance. Use small ones on bright days in clear water, and big ones when water is high or discolored so gamefish can see them more easily.

When conditions are bright and clear, many anglers use miniature streamers or bucktails—extremely slim, and only an inch or two long.

Steamers and bucktails fall into two classes—imitators and attractors. The imitators, such as the Pin Smelt, Black Nosed Dace and Sidewinder, are dressed in specific baitfish coloration, and they usually are the best ones to select. The attractors, such as the Mickey Finn, Royal Coachman and Black Ghost, are brighter colored with little or no resemblance to baitfish. While they are primarily dark-day and dirty-water flies, they are also taken by feeding fish under other conditions. Fish often rise to investigate them without taking. When this happens, switch to an imitator of the same size and work the fly over the fish again.

When a fish rises to a fly, it moves forward as well as upward, and then settles back into its holding position. Cast upstream of where the fish was seen so the fly has time to work into the fish's cone of vision at the proper depth.

Weedless Streamers And Bucktails

There are really two ways to make a fly hook weedless. One is to use Keel hooks, readily available from tackle stores and mail-order houses. In dressing the body, make sure the center of gravity allows the hook's bend to ride upward. The wing is dressed on the forward horizontal part of the hook so it encloses the barb. Keel flies in various sizes and patterns for fresh- or saltwater are available commercially. These flies can be cast into brush or weeds and dragged over lily pads and branches with rare hang-ups. When they first became available, there

The Figure Eight Turle Knot

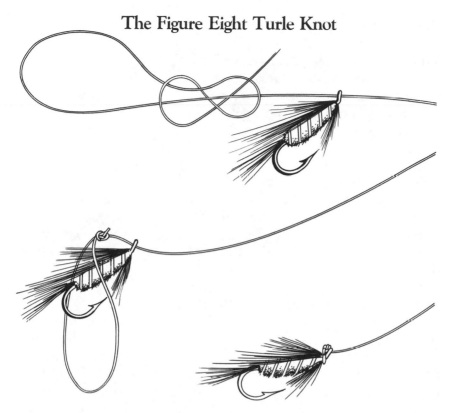

The Figure Eight Turle Knot is a quick way of securely attaching a fly to the tippet for fly fishing or to a light leader for spinning or spincasting presentations. This diagram shows the steps in tying the knot.

were some doubts about their hooking ability, but these seem to be unfounded. While hooking ability may be slightly inferior to conventional hooks, this is more than balanced by their excellence in negotiating weedy spots.

Conventional flies can be made weedless with a short piece of monofilament of suitable stiffness. When winding thread to start the body, wind it around both shank and monofilament, leaving a few inches of the monofilament protruding at the tail. Dress the body as usual. Bend the monofilament around and slightly outside the hook's bend and barb, tying it at the head.

The diameter or stiffness of the monofilament, of course, varies with the size of the fly. Use stiff material, if possible, and remember that it will soften somewhat when wet. This weedguard is almost invisible and can be concealed entirely by the underbody of the fly that is being used.

Weighted Streamers And Bucktails

Since gamefish are usually lying and feeding close to the bottom, flies that sink are often the most productive. Even fast-sinking lines may not get flies to drag bottom in fast currents. Weighting leaders or flies, or both, is often necessary. When weighting leaders, it is preferable to use several tiny split shot or lead strips rather than one large sinker. The shot or strips can be clamped to the leader just above one of the knots. Since this doesn't add to casting pleasure, weighted flies are a better solution. Use no more weight than necessary, and avoid confusion by segregating weighted patterns from unweighted ones in your fly box. One way is to dress or paint the heads a different color.

Making Fish Strike Steamers, Bucktails

A streamer or bucktail should be fished as a minnow swims—lazily turning while feeding on the bottom; drifting with the current; slowly swimming upstream, or suddenly darting away in panic. Four methods follow. You can experiment to find what works best at the time, and one can be combined with another. Fish often strike bucktails viciously, but sometimes they have to be teased into striking. Teasing works best when the lie of a big one is known.

The "swing retrieve" is used so often that many anglers don't realize there are other types of retrieves. Cast quartering upstream in a mild current, cross-stream in an average one, and quartering downstream when the flow is fast. First casts are made nearby and subsequent ones gradually extended to work the fly along feed lanes and into promising holding positions. As the fly works downstream, it travels across the current. No tip action is needed in fast current, but some is used when the current is mild to slow. If swift current causes the line to bag downstream, use upstream mends to keep the fly from whipping.

When no surface action is noted, you must keep the fly as deep as possible. This is accomplished by casting upstream and across, by using a sinking line, by weighting the fly or leader or by a combination of these methods. Keep the rod pointed at the fly and keep it low unless raising it is necessary to guide the fly through shallow water. Action is given when necessary by raising and lowering the rodtip. Try to make the swing at moderate speed, give it action when necessary, and guide it into places that look productive while keeping it as deep as possible.

When the fly has completed its swing, it hangs downstream. This is the time to give it prompt and vigorous action because fish often follow a fly and will take it when its action changes. Work it for 15 seconds or so by raising and lowering the rodtip. Recover it by the hand-twist retrieve.

In the "hand-twist retrieve" the cast is made directly downstream, or nearly so. This retrieve is made by turning the fingers of the line hand in order to collect small loops progressively in the palm as line is recovered. The action of the fly is supposed to imitate the slow progress of a baitfish working against the current. Line can be taken in and let out as desired to explore good holding positions.

This retrieve is excellent when the fly is cast downstream to swing in along an undercut bank or to maneuver it into spots like active eddies, near-shore edges and fallen trees.

This retrieve also is valuable when fancasting from a boat on a pond or lake, particularly in an inlet where a current is running. When there is no current, recovering the fly by slow stripping makes it more active.

While streamers and bucktails will take big fish all season long, they are particularly effective when fished deep and slowly during the run-offs of early spring when the trout are lying on bottom and feeding. Larger sizes with considerable glint are seen best when streams in spring are high and discolored. If you fish the fly at the proper level in the manner that a baitfish swims you should be confident of success. With sinking lines also use shorter leaders so the current won't sweep the fly up.

Although many streamers and bucktails made for trout also will take smallmouth and largemouth bass, bass have favorites that are somewhat different. Largemouth flies may have to be weedless. Some anglers have had excellent success with large, floppy multicolored streamers dropped crudely with a splat, allowed to sit on the surface a few moments, and then pulled under and fished in. Wooly Worms and Muddlers do well and can be fished in the same manner. Breather-type patterns such as marabous and splaywings also are excellent.

More Strikes With Wet Flies

Wet flies imitate winged insects which have drowned and are drifting in the current or which remain alive and are weakly trying to swim. Wet flies may imitate nymphs which have hatched into winged flies underwater just before emergence, or they may simulate winged flies of mayfly and caddis types which go underwater to lay eggs. Wet flies on occasion may also be taken for tiny baitfish, or unhatched nymphs.

Wet flies are the most venerable of all artificials. They were employed long before Dame Juliana Berners wrote about them in the 15th century and also before Charles Cotton added his section to Walton's *Compleat Angler* in the 17th. Early in this century, the advent of streamers and bucktails, and of dry flies and nymphs, relegated them to the background. This is a pity because modern tackle makes them more effective than ever. Many of us of the older generation learned fly fishing with them. They offer an extremely efficient way to take trout and other species which feed on insects.

One classic way to fish wet flies was to fasten three flies to a leader, making what was known as a "cast." This method is still popular in the British Isles. One is the point fly, at the end of the leader. The other two are dropper flies, tied to leader extensions between point and butt. (Check your local fishing regulations to determine if this method is legal on the water you're fishing.)

Casting Methods With Wet Flies

Since wet flies simulate dead insects, or live ones barely moving, they are usually drifted in currents or fished slowly in currentless water. Casts are planned to direct the flies through holding positions or feeding lanes, at the level of the fish, which normally is close to bottom.

One favorite method of fishing wet flies in streams is the "dead drift," as used with streamers, except that little, if any, action is given to the flies. The current does the work. Cast upstream and across to let the flies run deep and mend the line, upstream or downstream as necessary, to keep the cast at current speed. Small subcurrents work on one fly, which

Fishing Weighted Streamers

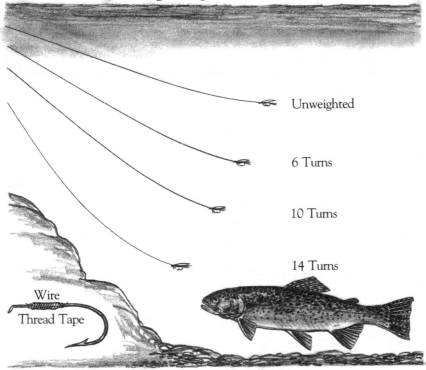

Weighted bodies get streamers down to the fish. The hook shank is wound tightly with No. 22 soft copper wire or lead fuse wire, tapered at each end with tying thread. Between six and 14 turns, depending on depth and current, are average.

activates the others in natural-appearing movement.

An exciting dividend when using more than one fly on a leader is that when they drift into a potential position a trout may grab one of them. Not to be outdone, another fish or two may strike the others. Conservation-minded anglers may question the ethics of multiple-fly use, but hopefully users will have "catch and release" in mind.

To fish the best wet fly patterns for local waters, check with a local tackle shop.

Nymphs

Nymph fishing, the "newest" of fly-rod methods, can be complicated for those who want to delve into its entomological aspects. Many successful nymph fishermen ignore most of the technical background and fish the way explained here. They maintain that the nymph pattern isn't all that important because anyone who grubs around in the silt and rocks of a stream always will find dozens of varieties of nymphs in all sizes and stages of development. The idea, they think, is to select an average-size artificial nymph—perhaps a gray one—and to learn to fish it properly, because presentation is more important than pattern.

Except under early-season, high-water conditions, trout take artificial nymphs very lightly, merely by picking them up. The most important part of nymph fishing is to learn to detect these very light takes and to tighten on the fish instantly. The signal usually is a slight pull on the line. To detect this more easily use a commercial strike indicator or wind the line-leader joint with fluorescent floss and varnish it. Bobbers for this purpose are so light and tiny that they can be cast without difficulty, but some prefer to mark the line-leader connection with a fluorescent color. While takes may be so light that they are almost imperceptible, high water conditions may make strikes much stronger, and fish may hook themselves when nymphs are drifting in strong currents, or even when the nymph is "dead" and lying nearly motionless on the bottom or hanging on completion of a swing.

If you ever forget to bring nymphs on the stream, take a wet fly with an appropriate body—a fuzzy one like a Hare's Ear or a Coachman—and cut off the wings, leaving a small nub to represent the wing pad. Wet-fly fishing and nymph fishing have many similarities. Casting methods are much the same.

Dry Flies

When emerging nymphs shed their skins on the water's surface, thus transforming themselves into flying insects, they must float there momentarily while their wings expand and harden. Fish wait near the surface in feeding lanes and holding positions and avidly suck in the helpless insects. Hatches occur during clement months, but usually in afternoon or evening when the sun has warmed the water. Then, anglers try to imitate whatever is emerging with artificials of the same size and appearance and enjoy added thrills of seeing their floating representations taken on the surface.

While dry-fly fishing is best during hatches, it may be good when there aren't any. If insect representations don't do well, try terrestrial ones like grasshoppers, ants and bees. You don't always need to be fussy about "matching the hatch" because a general representation often does as well as anything else if it is presented properly in suitable size. There are thousands of species and subspecies of flying insects which can be imitated, and hatches of several of them may occur at the same time. Thus a single general representation can take trout during any kind of hatch.

In dry-fly fishing, the line and fly should float and the leader should sink. Modern lines offer no floating problem if they are kept clean. Flies can be dried in the air, but spraying them with a flotant helps. There are preparations which make leaders sink, but soap, fish slime or mud can do it. The important thing is to use a properly tapered leader, 9 feet long, or more, with a tippet suitable in size to the fly. Coils can be removed by holding the leader taut and by rubbing it back and forth vigorously with a doubled piece of innertube rubber or a piece of soft leather to create frictional heat. Connect fly to leader with a Turtle knot.

Excellently matched tackle and the ideal choice of fly mean nothing if the cast is clumsy. Aim a few feet *above* the target so fly and leader will straighten and flutter down without splash. Also aim a few feet *upstream* of the target so the fly will drift into position. Also cast a few feet *beyond* the target so the rod can be pulled back a bit after the line has extended to make the line and leader drop in a series of S-curves to prevent drag during the drift. Drag can later be decreased by mending the line when necessary.

Upstream Casting

Upstream casting with the dry fly is the time-honored method, but you must cast a bit to the right or to the left so the leader won't pass over the fish. Since fish face upstream, your approach from behind is less obvious, particularly if you're wading with a low silhouette. The fly will drift toward you with minimum drag, and you must strip in line fast enough to be in control to strike a rising fish. The strip-in should never pull the fly. Since the strike is from downstream, with the fish facing upstream, the hook is pulled into the apex of the fish's jaws, where it should be. Another advantage of upstream fishing is that fish farther upstream are not disturbed.

Accomplished fly fishermen usually wait for rising fish and cast to selected ones. Of course, novices do that, too, but they also fish blindly, aiming casts so the fly will pass over or into potential holding positions or down feed lanes. Upstream casting can be any combination of up and across. When it is more across than up, drag on the fly can be postponed not only by checking the cast but also by wiggling the rod from side to side to shoot out extra line into a more pronounced series of S-curves. The line, of course, is mended as often as necessary.

Other suggestions for making fish strike: Get into the stream whenever possible, to maintain a low silhouette. Try to keep in position relative to the sun so your shadow won't disturb the fish. Fish and move slowly to minimize shock waves while in the water. When trout are rising out of reach, the nearer ones have heard or seen the angler because he isn't fishing slowly enough. Most fish can be taken within 30 feet. Too long a line only increases drag. When a trout rises but rejects the fly, this may be because of drag rather than incorrect pattern or size. A smaller fly may be needed. The leader tippet should be adjusted to the size of the fly. Don't avoid tying on finer tippets. If the leader piles up, it may need to be shortened.

In fast water, some favorite dry flies include the Rat Faced MacDougal and Irresistible, partly because of their superior floatability. Use the one you can see best. Wulff patterns also are excellent floaters. When fish are feeding in riffles, and when there is no reason for a different selection, try a Quill Gordon or a Light Cahill. In calm water, some favorites include the Blue Dun Spider and the Cream Variant, which is a spider with wings. Sizes 14 or 16 should be about right. Spiders are tied on bare hooks with very wide spade hackles from a rooster's throat—two hackles with concave sides together. It is hard to land them poorly because they are air-resistant and flutter down. They skate enticingly in the slightest breeze.

This brings up the suggestion that strikes often can be coaxed by putting life into the fly in calm water. When a fly has hatched and its wings have hardened, it rarely rises into the air directly. It runs on the water for takeoff speed much like a duck does, leaving a tiny wake behind. This can be simulated, and

Complete Angler's Library

Here's a brown trout that was eager to take an artificial fly that resembled what was food in his particular stream.

trout seem to go for flies that are trying to escape. Some insects, such as stone flies, are swimmers whose action can be duplicated to simulate the living insect. Terrestrials, including grasshoppers, ants and bees, swim on the surface. An excellent way to trigger strikes is to cast a Muddler dry so it floats, and to make it swim like a grasshopper with tiny twitches of the rodtip. If a lunker lies below it should come for it.

Downstream Casting

While upstream dry-fly fishing is the traditional method, it is often more convenient to fish downstream. Wind direction or the sun's position may influence this. Wading downstream requires less exertion than trying to wade up, and fast water may make it mandatory. Casts nearly downstream present the fly without the fish seeing the leader. Many positions can be fished downstream much better than up. We read the water and decide each situation on its merits.

Downstream casting, of course, requires more loose line to obtain a suitable float, and it may require mending the line frequently. (Because current in the middle of a stream is faster than at the sides, the heavier fly line may travel "faster" than the tippet and fly, thus creating a "drag" on the fly. This can be corrected by lifting the fly line from the water and swinging or "mending" it back upstream so that the heavier fly line "trails" the fly going downstream.) Pulling back on the rod as the cast straightens out lands the line in S-curves which provide a short float without drag, and shaking out more line also may be necessary.

Downstream fishing is at its best in slow-flowing water. An ideal situation then may be a combination of both up and down, such as to cover a run along an undercut bank or the upstream side of a submerged rock and the edges below it. Aim the cast quartering upstream and mend while the fly works downstream, providing additional line as needed.

Dry Fly On Fast Water

Many smaller streams run fast, but big trout, especially rainbows, can abound in them. Light tackle is preferable because thick lines offer greater water resistance and thus tend to drag, or pull on the fly. Since casts must be short because of the broken currents, a double-tapered line is preferable to a forward-tapered one. Light tackle with light lines permit using lighter leaders for freer fly movement and less drag. This light tackle, with short casts, still allows wading anglers to probe many holding positions, perhaps all of them on the smaller streams. When rivers are wider and also very fast, the dry fly may be unsuitable.

Casts in fast water must be short and frequent. Long leaders help to keep flies floating. The sneaky approach is less important because the disturbed surface obscures anglers from fish. The rough surface also decreases fly visibility, making pattern less important but increasing the necessity for color contrast. Rocky stretches offering promising edges and holding water can probably be fished most effectively by working upstream, but downstream fishing should usually be more practical.

Of course, dry flies for fast water must have extreme buoyancy to float high. Wulff patterns and those with clipped deer-hair bodies are ideal. They will often be pulled under but the cast can then be completed wet.

Bass Bugs And Similar Floaters

In addition to flies, artificials for the fly rod include a vast and potent array of deer-hair, cork and plastic floaters excellent for bass, surface-feeding panfish and even pike and muskies. Lunker trout (especially brown trout) shouldn't be excluded, particularly when you fish for them at night. These lures include lightweight poppers of many sorts and sizes as well as representations of mice, frogs, moths, bugs and anything else landing on the surface which fish consider suitable for dinner.

Depending on the size and air-resistance of the lure, rods can vary in size—from lightweight rods taking line size 6 to heavier ones taking size 10. Since all of these lures are air-resistant to some degree, a weight-forward floating line is needed to cast them properly. For the big lures, a bass-bug taper, made particularly for the purpose, should be chosen. You can be less particular about the leader for casting the bigger lures, but it should be about as long as the rod and should gradually taper from about 12 to 8 pounds. A strong tippet is needed to turn the bulky lures over, and is acceptable because the fish with which you are concerned are less fussy than trout. A strong leader is required because much of this fishing is amid lily pads, grasses, stumps, brush and other obstructions from which hooked fish must be pulled quickly. Weedless hooks are usually valuable.

Popping lures are fished by allowing them to lie quietly after the cast, then given noisy pops and gurgles by pulling the rodtip back sharply. This noise and surface commotion wakes up lethargic bass and usually elicits lusty strikes.

Except for poppers and bullet heads, nearly all of these lures imitate naturals. In addition to casting the lures to potential hotspots, you must work the lure exactly as its live counterpart swims; *don't hurry or overdo it.*

Big bass love mice. Big trout do, too. Little gray or black

fly-rod mice with bodies only an inch or so long plus a rubberband tail are made of closely cropped deer body hair, and therefore very buoyant. Mice often fall off logs, or try to swim from one place to another. Unlike frogs, they paddle steadily but very slowly on the surface, leaving small, enticing wakes. Fish the lure steadily and slowly, perhaps with a few pauses.

Due in part to insecticides, moths are less prevalent than they used to be, but bass don't seem to realize that. A moth flutters steadily over the surface, like a float plane getting speed for takeoff. Fly-rod moths are made of cropped deer hair, with wide and long horizontal wings. Fish them with the mouse treatment, but perhaps a little faster.

These four fly-rod artificials are all that seems necessary for largemouth bass, and smallmouths may take the same lures in smaller sizes. If they don't, they may not be in the shallows, and you'll have to look for them in deeper structure. Bass habitually move into the shallows to feed between dusk and dawn when the water is in a temperature range comfortable for swimming. In some regions, particularly in the South, they may be in the shallows most of the time.

Smallmouth bass fishing is more akin to trouting than to largemouth fishing, partly because smallmouths shun weedy places for rocky or gravely ones. Their diet is insects and their nymphs, terrestrials such as moths, beetles and hoppers, crayfish and small baitfish. Since insects which have fallen into the water are drifted by winds to the windward shore, the feeding pattern of smallmouths is more pronounced.

Thus, smallmouths take fly-rod lures which have been mentioned for trout. There are two favorite floaters for them. One is the ever-popular Muddler Minnow fished dry, like a grasshopper, or a real grasshopper imitation. Another is a deer-hair bug, such as the Cooper Bug. It can be deadly for rising smallmouths when fished properly. This means to land it delicately and to let it sit without motion for nearly a minute. Then, give it just the faintest twitch, followed by a few more. If there are no takers, pick it up and drop it in another place. Here again the imitation must be fished as the natural would act. Rubber bugs, caterpillars, grubs, ants, bees and tiny popping lures also are excellent floaters for smallmouths and for many other panfish. Good hook sizes are from No. 4 to No. 6.

Bluegills (bream) are favorites among the panfish which feed on insects. Try them with light fly rods and fine leaders using any of the midget-sized lures. Best results come when the little lures are fished along shorelines with cover in early morning or during the evening when the sun is off the water. You may have to experiment to find out which type of lure takes best at any one time, but that is part of the fun. Whatever it is, the secret is to fish it as its living counterpart would act if it were on the water.

16

Using Natural Baits In Streams And Lakes

Fly fishermen and bait addicts don't always agree. Fly fishermen often scorn the use of bait as unsportsmanlike, while bait fishermen maintain that the point is to catch fish and have fun.

When streams are cold, high and discolored, the angler who can drift a worm (or other bait) along the bottom into a good holding position usually scores while those who use flies, plugs or metal lures don't do too well. Later in the season, when conditions are right, artificials do best, one of the reasons being that the lure is in the water more often.

While everyone is entitled to their opinion, it doesn't pay to be dogmatic. Try all methods and find the ones most satisfying. In the 17th century, Izaak Walton, a bait fisherman, befriended Charles Cotton, who preferred artificial flies. Each respected the other's opinions and both remain famous today.

Some natural baits do better under certain conditions or for specific species of fish than do others. Some baits are available when others are not. There are different ways to rig and fish each kind of bait.

Tackle For Baitfishing

While experienced bait fishermen may become wedded to one method or another, there are guidelines for more strikes.

For fishing streams, consider the advantages of the fly rod. A short, light rod can be poked through foliage along small

This nice bass was taken on a shiner minnow that was allowed to roam a weedbed beneath a balloon used as a float.

Using Natural Baits In Streams And Lakes

streams where a short drift of the bait into good holding positions may be all that is necessary or possible. When lack of obstructions permits flipping baits longer distances, a longer and stronger fly rod is preferable; in wide streams, the longer the better. With added length you can guide the bait down feed lanes on either side of your position, reaching out to work it around rocks, guiding it into obstructions such as fallen trees, or probing the hotspots below undercut banks. The advantages of the long rod, as compared to shorter spinfishing or spinning gear, is illustrated by the fact that some experts in America, and many in Europe, use rods (or poles) as long as 12 feet or more to guide baits more accurately. The tackle and tactics for this kind of fishing will be discussed later.

While the fly rod has decided advantages in small to medium-sized streams, it is much less valuable in really wide ones. Here, spinning gear is better because longer casts are necessary to sweep baits down wide stretches and to fish them near the bottom of deep pools and runs where prize fish so often lie. The finer diameter monofilament lines also drag less and drift baits more naturally after long casts. The choice between spinning, spincasting or baitcasting gear is more or less a personal one.

At first glance, using the fly rod for baitfishing seems only as simple as putting a worm on a hook and drifting it into a likely lie. Those who habitually hook trophy trout know there is more to it than that. Let's see how they do it. The three methods are all effective depending on conditions.

The Fly Rod With A Floating Line
This method is similar to, but more precise than the usual way of using fly rods for baitfishing which anglers have been employing for many generations. Knowledgeable water readers will find that it brings more strikes from bigger fish. It is particularly adaptable for fast streams and provides excellent results in the high water run-offs of the early season.

All we need is a long fly rod (8 to 9½ feet) with a standard reel and a double-tapered floating line. Attach a level leader (regular monofilament of about 4-pound test) to the line with a nail or nail-less knot or a leader whip knot. The leader should be at least as long as the rod. The knot must be smooth enough to pass through the guides easily, and it helps to coat it with fluorescent paint for noting strikes.

Tie a small, short-shanked hook to the leader's end, remembering that it should be unobtrusive and buried in the bait as far as possible consistent with hooking ability. Add a bit of lead about a foot and a half above the hook, and perhaps another bit or two spaced farther up on the leader. The kind and amount of lead is important.

My favorite lead is the twist-on strips about the shape of paper book matches, readily available in folders like common match books. Tear off a strip, cut it in two, and wrap half a strip on the leader, perhaps using the other half farther up. Wound around the leader neatly, with ends crimped, the strips rarely catch on anything. Other leads, such as split shot, can be used, but I don't consider them as good.

The right amount of lead is of primary importance to work bait near bottom without its catching too frequently. Use enough small bits of spaced lead to get the bait down, but remove a little if it catches. If catch-ups are chronic anyway (as happens on very rocky streams) the alternative is to tie in a short dropper and to add to its end a pinch-on lead or two which can be pulled off if they become snagged. This is similar to what steelhead anglers do when they use a pencil lead on a dropper lighter than the line.

This rig can be cast upstream, downstream or cross-stream. When casting upstream, the line must be retrieved fast enough to keep it tight. You can follow the progress of the bait by watching the floating line. When the line hesitates during a drift, strike quickly. Of course, the bait must be drifted at current speed regardless of the direction it is fished. Use only enough lead to fish the bait on or near bottom, and maintain line control so you can feel a strike.

When fishing with this rig, sometimes the bait sinks and won't drift naturally in slow runs or pools. A natural drift can be achieved by using a small, light sponge-rubber bobber. This type is less of an impediment to casting than most, but still it should be used only when necessary. The bobber should be only large enough to hold up the bait so that when a fish takes the lure it feels little or no resistance. If, when a fish strikes, the bobber jerks back, the fish quickly discovers that the bait is unnatural and usually the fish will refuse it.

While a floating line is superior for most stream fishing, a floating one with a sinking tip may be advisable for deep water. Avoid sinking lines, however; they make it difficult to feel and handle strikes.

Spinning or spincasting reels can also be used with the fly rod; they are more convenient for fishing downstream. Since the reel is on the grip behind the hand, this may seem awkward at first, but awkwardness disappears with experience. In downstream fishing, either type of reel can release line as freely as the current takes the bait to provide a natural drift. Line can be controlled by the forefinger of the rod hand, and can be snubbed by it when the angler wants to strike or to hold the lure in position. The line can be put under control of the reel instantly, whereupon the fish is handled as usual with the type of reel being used. This method combines the line control afforded by a spinning reel with the pleasure of playing a fish on a fly rod.

Longer rods aid you in guiding baits where you want them to go. The idea is ancient, but often ignored by modern fishermen. Old books illustrate rods 16 feet or even longer, used for precise placement and drifting of baits. While this was the main reason for them, lack of adequate reels was another. The idea continues in cane-pole fishing, but you may not realize that light fiberglass poles about 12 feet long, equipped with tiny spool-like reels holding only a small quantity of monofilament, are not uncommon on some trout streams today. Users extend only about 5 or 6 feet of line from the rodtip, drop the slightly weighted bait into a run, and fish it down by swinging the long pole at current speed to get perfect drifts with the bait bouncing bottom. These anglers often catch big fish that are the envy and astonishment of anglers using other methods. Izaak Walton used the same technique in the 17th century, and others did before him. In some respects, angling hasn't changed very much!

Spinning And Spincasting Hints

Some confusion still exists between spinning and spincasting. These two methods are quite different.

The spinning reel has an open face and a fixed spool from

Tying A Nail-Less Knot

This is basically the fly fisherman's standard nail knot without the nail. Wrap the lighter monofilament leader around the heavier fly line as shown and be sure to trim the tag ends for a nice, smooth knot.

which the line spirals off unimpeded until slowed down or stopped by forefinger pressure and closing the bail. Rods have large ring guides to aid smooth outflow of line and they are moderately stiff for accurate, long-distance casting. Lack of drag, allows longer casts with lighter lines and lures.

The spincasting reel, on the other hand, has a closed face from which the line peels off to pass through a small hole in the center of the spool's cover, or hood. This adds considerable friction but eliminates excess line spiraling off prematurely, causing snarls. Rods are shorter than those used in spinning, and are similar to baitcasting rods. Thus, to get much distance in spincasting, we must use heavier lures.

The spincasting method is considered more foolproof for novices, but the longer casts with lighter lines and lures (or baits) strongly recommends spinning. There's more to it than that. Fishermen who habitually use lures which should be retrieved erratically, and who often fish in dense cover, should choose spinning tackle. Success with spinning tackle requires that the line be retrieved under fairly constant tension to pack it smoothly on the reel spool. It is difficult to do this when using surface popping plugs or other lures that are bucktailed on the retrieve.

Worm Fishing With Fixed-Spool Tackle

With spinning and spincasting tackle, somewhat heavier terminal tackle—baits, leads and floats—is needed. These help us to fish deeper, at the right temperature levels.

The most successful worm fishermen don't dig and use their bait the same day. They let them lie in moss, damp leaves or commercial worm bedding long enough to scour themselves of ingested dirt and body slime. This leaves them a bright pink or red and tougher and livelier on the hook. Remember to use small, short-shank hooks which can be concealed in the bait as much as possible, hooking worms only once, through the collar.

Drift the worm naturally with the current into holding positions, leaving the pickup open so line can peel off the reel. The outflow is controlled by forefinger pressure on spinning reels and by finger and thumb pressure on spincasting reels. On a strike, the line can quickly be put under control of the reel. There is a bit of an art to releasing line properly and still feeling strikes, but this is easily learned. When enough line has been released, put it under control of the reel and let the lure hang downstream momentarily. A fish following it might then pick it up. Retrieve it slowly, through edges and holding positions.

Although it isn't natural for worms to travel upstream, their appearance and smell may make hungry fish forget this. Fishing a worm upstream can be more productive than fishing downstream or quartering downstream. By casting upstream or quartering upstream, the bait drifts down naturally and bumps bottom in fast currents. The trick is to retrieve all slack line without pulling the bait, except when necessary to guide it above a target so it will drift down into it. If the bait lodges on bottom in slower currents, a tighter line may be needed to keep it off gravel or rocks.

Bobbers are helpful for fishing worms in deep pools and runs; also in ponds and lakes. When a bobber is set far up on the line, it is difficult to cast. A small button can be used as a bobber stop (many commercial bobber stops are available). String the button on the monofilament; string on the sliding bobber, and add a split shot or two a foot or so above the bait. In casting, the bobber is against the split shot, so it doubles as a casting weight. In the water, the bait and shot sink and the bobber rises up the line to be stopped at the button. The button can be slid along the monofilament to regulate depth. Of course, this rig can be used with minnows and other baits.

A bobber is used to suspend bait at a desired depth. It is not needed in currents fast enough to carry bait, but is helpful in drifting bait down a languid pool, or over a weedy bottom.

How To Fish Nightcrawlers

Anglers who use nightcrawlers may have noticed that, after a cast or two, the bait is doubled unnaturally on the hook. Fish rarely take it in this condition. The bait must look natural and must drift naturally for best results. Use bright, well scoured crawlers and replace them when they become inactive. Use small, short-shanked hooks, concealed in the bait as much as possible. When water conditions permit, let the bait drift and sink naturally, without lead, or keep weight to a minimum.

There are two effective rigs for nightcrawlers. In the first, the small, short-shanked hook is buried in the head of the worm, rather than through the collar. This allows the bait to act more naturally, but it also encourages bait stealers. If lead is necessary, many prefer the twist-on type (discussed earlier) about 18 inches above the bait.

When small, bait-stealing fish are not present, this is the best rig. Fish it on a taut line so you can feel taps. When a fish starts to take the bait, give it line and delay setting the hook until you guess the bait has been ingested. Then strike hard; the crawler may be wrapped around the hook and the barb must penetrate it to set in the fish's jaw.

When small, bait-stealing fish make this single-hook rig impractical, use a tandem rig shown. When lead must be used, a good arrangement is to tie a very small swivel into the line about 18 inches above the hook, with a sliding sinker above it.

The swivel prevents the sinker from sliding down to the bait. The two hooks allow you to strike quicker. Use short-shanked hooks, about size No. 8.

Salmon Eggs

The best eggs are taken from freshly killed Pacific salmon or steelhead trout when they are ready to spawn. In salmon or steelhead rivers some spawned but uncovered eggs drift downstream and are eagerly sought by fish of all species, even in other rivers where spawning does not occur.

When fresh eggs are not available, preserved ones are acceptable and are readily found in tackle stores everywhere. Since the use of eggs as bait is prohibited in some states, check your local regulations before using them.

Fishing With Minnows

Minnows can be fished properly with any light tackle. Most anglers use spinning or spincasting gear, but old-timers still prefer a fly rod for stream fishing, and for good reason. As with worm fishing, the longer rod can guide the bait into good holding positions with a minimum of line drag.

There are many ways to rig minnows. Live ones can be hooked upward through both lips or under the forward part of the dorsal fin "above" the backbone. They are especially effective when tipping a jig.

Of course, minnows that have expired are used, and even preserved ones will do. The bait stays on the hook until a fish mashes it. Let the bait roll and drift into good holding positions, but give it slight action with the rodtip in imitation of a baitfish in distress. This rig is also excellent for trolling.

Another efficient rig can be made with a double hook. The only tool needed is a long needle. If you're lacking one, bend a tiny loop in one end of a few inches of stiff stainless-steel wire. Thread several inches of monofilament line or leader through the loop (or needle's eye) and push the point into the minnow's mouth through the body and out the vent. With the bait strung on the monofilament, tie a double hook to its end. Push the shank into the bait's vent and body until it is buried there, and tighten the monofilament. The hook's barbs straddle the bait.

When streams are cold, the baits which have been discussed

Harnessing Live Bait

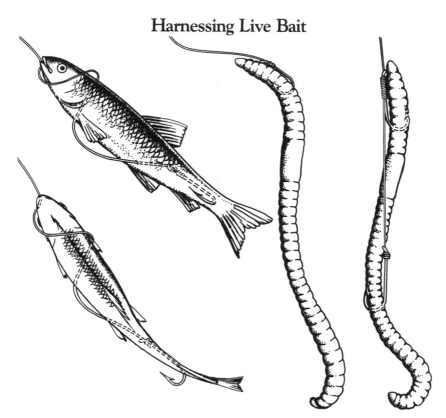

This diagram shows on the left co-author Bates' method for "sewing" a minnow on a hook to prevent bait stealing. At right are two rigs for fishing nightcrawlers. One produces maximum action and the other (far right) is again intended to prevent bait stealing.

must bounce bottom where the fish usually are. One way to do this is to use enough lead on the line above the bait to take it down in the current. This usually requires an upstream cast, or one quartering upstream. The trick is to keep slack out of the line then, so you can feel the bait bouncing bottom, keep it moving, and also feel strikes.

Another method is borrowed from steelhead fishermen. Tie a small, three-way swivel to the line's end. Attach the bait to a foot or more of leader and tie this to one of the swivel's rings. Attach a split shot or a pencil lead to about half the above amount of leader and fasten this to the third swivel ring. The monofilament which attaches the lead should be considerably weaker than the line so it will break when badly snagged. The strength of the monofilament to which the bait is attached should be between the other two. Hang-ups sometimes are frequent, but all you usually lose is the lead. If the bait snags and can't be pulled loose, it is usually broken at the swivel or at the hook. Remember the old maxim that you aren't fishing deep enough if the bait doesn't snag occasionally, so carry plenty of lead, leaders and hooks. Pencil weights snag the least. Keep the line tight so the bouncing lead can be felt as your twitching rodtip guides it. This rig is often used in trolling when fish are lying on bottom.

Another simple way to hook a minnow for casting is shown in the drawing on page 164. You need a few short-shanked bait hooks, in sizes 1 or 1/0 and preferably offset or double offset. Attach a hook to about a foot of monofilament and attach the monofilament to the line with a small barrel swivel. Run the hook's point into the mouth and out one of the gills. Then, turn the hook and push it completely through the body back of the head. Let point and barb emerge.

The bait should be given slight rodtip action unless the current is strong. Fish it upstream, or up and across, keeping slack line reeled in so strikes can be felt. If the strike is light, allow momentary slack before setting the hook to allow the fish to take the bait solidly. The first method is preferable for trolling because the rig has built-in action. All can be used for trolling or casting, but the second and third methods work best when action is imparted to the lure.

Leeches: Hardy Tempters

Leeches abound in lakes, ponds and slow-moving streams across North America. Though there are many types of leeches, only the ribbon leech is widely used by anglers.

Leeches make excellent bait, especially for walleyes, smallmouth bass, bluegills and other species. They are easy to keep and writhe constantly when hooked, enticing fish even during the mid-summer months when other forage is plentiful.

Crayfish: Sometimes The Best Bait

Part of the fun of fishing is to visit new places and to learn the methods other anglers use. In some spots, the usually popular worms and minnows are spurned because the name of the game there is "crayfish." Call them what you will—

crawfish, crawdads or lobsters, among other names—the crayfish during its season is considered by many to be the best bait of all. Small ones take smallmouths; bigger ones tempt largemouths. Trout, walleyes, catfish and perch will grab any crayfish they can get their jaws around.

You won't find crayfish in all waters because some lack proper alkalinity for them to grow and shed their shells properly. Some states prohibit the use of crayfish for bait, so check local laws before fishing. Crayfish can be caught in traps (like lobster traps) baited with fish or fish-based cat food. Use a quarter-inch nylon seine to gather them in brooks. Let it bag downstream and scuff rocks above to dislodge the crayfish and drive them into the net.

Use short-shanked hooks about No. 6 for small crayfish, and up to No. 2 for bigger ones. One way to hook them is upward through the tail; another, which may keep them alive longer, is to push the hook's point from the rear forward under some of the tail's segments. It is important that the bait be fresh or it will be ignored, so replace it after every few casts.

Crayfish can be kept alive in cool water that is changed frequently. Since they fight each other, and can nip rather painfully, the larger ones should be declawed. To do this, grasp the pincher with fishing pliers; the crayfish will shake off its claw. (It will grow another if it lives.)

How do you fish crayfish? Suppose you are fishing in summer for bass in a lake where they inhabit structure just below the thermocline, which is at about 30 feet. Use spinning or spincasting tackle with about 6-pound-test line, no sinker. Hook the crayfish as explained above, and cast about 30 feet. The bait will try to swim down, going in a quarter circle from the surface to below the boat. Keep the reel's bail open to give line. You'll feel taps when a fish takes, but let it run because it will pause to swallow the bait tailfirst. That's the time to strike—hard!

Crayfish can be used for smallmouths, trout and walleyes. They try to crawl under rocks, so pull gently on the line to keep them moving where fish can smell and see them.

Hellgrammites
The popular hellgrammite is a mean-looking dark-brown or

black water inhabitant which is the larval form of the dobsonfly, sometimes misnamed dragonfly. It has six pairs of legs plus various little claws and feelers and a pair of nippers in front which can bite. It reaches a length of about 3 inches and can be found under rocks in and near streams.

Frequently, during a lull in noonday fly fishing, anglers have turned over a wet rock, grabbed a slithering hellgrammite, hooked it under the collar, tossed it into a likely run, and caught the biggest trout of the day. These little wigglers are so tough on a hook that one may take several fish. They are also excellent bait for smallmouth bass, walleye and various other fish. If you want to collect a few, they can be carried in a can of damp rotted leaves or moss. Use small, short-shanked hooks. Slip the point under the hard collar just back of the head, or hook them through the tail. Under the collar is best. Let them drift into holding positions as you would fish garden worms. If they reach bottom, they will try to hide under rocks, so keep them drifting.

Grasshoppers

Everyone knows the familiar grasshopper found in fields in summer and early fall, but not everyone realizes it is an excellent surface bait for trout, smallmouth bass and panfish. On cold mornings, they can easily be picked off their grassy perches in fields. On warm days, when they are too active to catch that way, lay a blanket over the grass and chase the hoppers onto it. Their feet will catch in the fluff of the blanket where they can be picked off. Carry them in a box with a sliding cover which contains pieces of nylon stockings to which the hoppers will adhere.

The best way to hook a grasshopper is under the collar back of the neck. Use a short-shank, light-wire hook. To keep it alive on the hook, don't impale it but wrap a very small rubber band a couple of turns around its body just forward of the long hopping legs, and slip the hook's point under the bands. Chronic hopper users solder two short lengths of fine wire crossway on a hook shank, one under the point and the other farther back. Then hold the hopper on the shank with its head under the bend and twist each of the two wires together lightly around the body.

If you don't want to try to trap crickets, they're available as indicated here in preserved form. Use of preserved baits has been gaining in popularity.

When fishing a hopper, let it drift on or just under the surface. A fly rod and a floating line are the best tackle, but you can also use spinning or spincasting gear with a floating bubble a foot or so up the line.

Crickets And Nymphs

Black or dark-brown crickets are common in summer in fields and even in damp cellars. Look for them under rocks, boards and tar paper. They can be baited with bread or crumbs. Catch, keep and hook them like grasshoppers. The harnessing method is best because they are rather fragile and easy to cast off the hook. They are excellent bait for trout, bass and panfish.

If you turn over rocks or pull up masses of rotting vegetation in a stream you'll find nymphs of various kinds and sizes. Big ones can be strung on light-wire hooks or can be hooked in back of the head. The wire harness can also be used with very small hooks. These nymphs of course eventually emerge to shuck their nymphal skins to transform themselves into flying insects. Some, like the stone fly nymph of Western waters, grow very large and are greatly favored as baits. Those who want to study nymphs and to dress artificials to represent them will find many excellent books on the subject. Suffice it to say that any that are big enough to put on a hook make excellent baits for trout, smallmouth bass and many other fish species. Carry them for fishing in a small box containing damp moss or leaves.

Mealworms And Grubs

Catalpa worms, found in season on catalpa trees in the South, are popular baits for bluegills and other panfish, and they are typical of many worms, caterpillars and grubs which can be strung on light-wire hooks to catch trout, smallmouth bass and various panfish. The white grubs of the June bug and the Japanese beetle are frequently found while digging in the garden. Fishermen in desperate need of bait should notice the round galls on dry goldenrod stalks. When split open, they usually yield a small grub.

Anglers have found that smooth-skinned caterpillars are good bait, but not furry ones. Their taste repels fish.

Cut Bait

Finally, when you've caught a fish or two, remember that strips of belly, eyeballs and even the fins make good bait, on a plain hook or on a spinner, spoon, jig or crankbait. Just cut a strip of fish belly of appropriate size and hook it at one end. The strips can be cut in various shapes; it's fun to experiment. (Again, check local regulations.)

Locating Fish

Bass And Panfish

W hen fishermen talk about bassin' and panfishing, it's like two different worlds coming together, although a lot of bass fishing waters are popular panfish waters, as well. Perhaps no other sportfish has as much time, effort and money, in terms of fishing crafts and tackle, devoted to it as do bass. Panfish, however, are often considered "starter" fish—something you catch as a kid learning the sport and then graduate to "real" fish like largemouth or smallmouth bass.

This chapter is designed to give NAFC members a quick introduction to finding both bass and the "major" panfish species—crappies, bluegills and perch—to further enhance members' enjoyment of catching all these species. They're all scrappy, fun to catch and there's good eating in it for you, too.

Locating Largemouth Bass

The first step in catching largemouth bass is finding active fish. And while this can be difficult at times, there are many shortcuts you can take on the road to success, especially if you know a little about bass biology and habits. This will help you eliminate unproductive water, and focus your efforts in areas likely to be holding fish.

Bass spawn when inshore waters reach about 60 degrees (March to June, depending on location) in weedy sand or gravel areas only a few feet deep. They clean out a roundish bed and

These anglers knew where to find fish. They headed for the shallows and the bass were there, ready for a fight.

Bass And Panfish

make them slightly dish-shaped, depositing eggs near the center. These beds are easily spotted, active ones being guarded by a bass. This is easy fishing because almost any lure, dragged slowly over a bass bed, will be struck by the fish. He does this from anger, rather than from hunger, in order to get the intruder out of the way.

Many anglers disapprove of fishing during the spawn because of the potential harm it does. Catching a male fish off a spawning bed leaves the nest susceptible to egg-eating panfish, which can empty a nest in a matter of minutes. Seasons for some species are closed during their spawning.

We know that feeding areas for largemouth bass include relatively shallow stretches, usually near shore, which contain an abundance of grasses, weeds, lily pads and other vegetation which usually grow above the water. These feeding areas have an escape or migratory route to deeper water, such as a deep drop-off nearby. A grassy but narrow shoreline also containing logs and brush is ideal bass habitat, especially when connected to a drop-off. This type of spot can also be a spawning area. Other feeding areas may be vast expanses of lily pads, water hyacinths or stump ranches.

In lakes with deep water, bass spend most of their time in the structure we have described. They usually leave them near dusk for shallow feeding areas and remain there until the sun and warming water induce them to return the next morning—early if the sun is bright and later if it isn't. In deep water, they seek a hard rather than a muddy bottom—a difference that can be seen on sonar.

Many anglers believe bass shun sunlight. Bright light, they say, dazzles bass because, like most fish, they have no eyelids and their pupils can't expand and contract to protect their eyes from glare. Otherwise, there would be no reason, beyond seeking suitable water temperatures, for leaving their feeding areas at all. As it is, they are driven from them to deeper structure to escape sunlight.

This provides a few hints for finding bass in shallow-water feeding areas. Don't look for them when the sun is bright, but they may linger longer in the shallows on dark days. When the sun is out and you want to fish the shallows, the best fishing will be in the shade; on the eastern sides of lakes in early

With a belly boat, an angler can sneak up on bass as this California angler did with this 6-pound, 9-ounce largemouth in the Highland Springs (California) Reservoir.

morning and on the western sides in the afternoon.

The relative turbidity of water also should be considered. Some shore areas are very discolored by decomposition of vegetation and perhaps by runoff water. Bass stay in such places longer, and may remain in relatively shallow potholes more or less permanently. They also may remain in areas dense with large lily pads, which act as umbrellas to shade them from sun.

Experts maintain that when anglers face shallow water to fish for bass 90 percent of the fish are behind them—that is, in deeper structure. Also bass in the shallows are scattered rather than concentrated in schools of similarly sized fish in the productive "honey holes" so often found by people who understand structure fishing.

While this may be so, many anglers prefer fishing the

shallows because of the challenge of casting accurately into openings in the weeds or along their edges. They prefer the thrill of seeing a big bass smash a lure on top to the tamer experience of a deep-water strike. They often prefer to wade, and find it comfortable in warm weather to do so unencumbered by waders. They know that wading anglers can get closer to bass without spooking them than can those fishing from boats. When weedlines are deep, wading anglers can use float tubes to drift into areas that are over their heads.

Shallow-water fishing is best in spring when waters are cool and bass are spawning. Productive lures are surface plugs, crankbaits, spinnerbaits and weedless plastic worms. Later spring calls for deep-water lures; plastic worms inched along the bottom, jig and pig combinations, and spinnerbaits fished slowly. Jigs with pork-rind tails attached are usually recovered with sweeping and twitching motions of the rodtip. Spinnerbaits do best in shallow water when repeatedly allowed to flutter down on a nearly slack line and then jerked up. Thick cover along banks (including entering streams and ditches), drop-offs around islands, points of land and the backs of coves amid cover are usually productive then. In summer, bass are usually in deep holes and other deep structure during daylight, but also may be found in shallow springs and cold-water feeders. In the fall, bass return to the flats more often, and cloudy midday fishing should be good, especially in shallows on the edge of deep water.

Many of us who prefer to hook bass on top like to do it with sturdy fly rods. Streamer flies do well, particularly colorful and floppy ones. These can be made weedless by dressing the hook with a loop of strong monofilament edging bend and barb. Leaders should test at least 10 pounds, and perhaps as much as 20 or so because, once hooked, the fish must be kept on top and skidded in over the surface to open water to avoid tangles.

Smallmouth Bass

Though generally smaller than the largemouth, the smallmouth bass gets many votes in the "scrappiest, pound for pound" category. The two species are somewhat similar in appearance, but the jaw of a smallmouth does not extend beyond a line perpendicular to the eye; the largemouth's does.

Although the two bass have many similarities, it is the differences that are important. Both species follow similar migratory routes from feeding shallows to cooler and deeper sanctuaries, but many smallmouths remain in the depths year-round which makes their dusk-to-dawn feeding habits similar when they migrate to the shallows. Both spawn in shallow water near shore, but smallmouths make smaller and neater nests. Smallmouths—especially the bigger ones—spawn around exposed islands and on or near submerged ones.

Spawning takes place between late April and late June, depending on the region, when water temperatures reach about 60 degrees. Like largemouths, smallmouths on spawning beds will strike at almost anything. This is a good time for fly fishing with barbless hooks. On tight lines, very few fish get away.

Smallmouths are fussier than largemouths about water temperatures; only a few degrees make a difference in their habitats or cruising levels. Optimum temperatures are between 59 and 65 degrees in northern regions and between 60 and 72 degrees in the South.

In Lakes

In deep water, which means about 30 feet, depending on temperature and clarity, smallmouths are found over rocky or gravel bottoms, usually where there is little or no vegetation. A favorite spot is a rock face, or rocky cliff, with boulders strewn on the bottom. Sometimes waterlogged timber clutters such places, but the fish cruise in plain sight, ignoring anglers peering down from boats above, evidently feeling safe in the security of depth and quick access to rocky hideaways.

Rocky drop-offs are equally good, as well as rocky or gravel points of land. Rocky islands and submerged mounds are excellent when anglers fish their lures at proper temperature depths. Submerged ledges also should pay off.

Proper fishing depth is a combination of optimum temperatures and light penetration, which is influenced by the relative turbidity of water. When it's clear, fish deep; when it's turbid, fish shallow. Fish may be at their higher optimum levels when the surface is disturbed by wind, but they will be much deeper when the surface is glassy—or the shade of rocks and debris.

Smallmouth bass, like largemouths, migrate from the depths

of lakes to shallow feeding areas, particularly between dusk and daylight. Crayfish, when present, are their favorite food, but they often dash out from schools to snatch small baitfish. In gravel areas, they nose the bottom in search of crayfish and nymphs. When hatches are on they feed like trout, taking emerging mayflies, stone flies and caddis flies on the surface. They also feed on worms, nightcrawlers, leeches, hellgrammites and small frogs. Smallmouths feed on the surface when water temperatures reach about 65 degrees.

In the Thousand Islands area of the St. Lawrence River, fishermen habitually catch smallmouths on bait. They use spinning or spincasting tackle with a 2-inch live baitfish hooked under the dorsal fin or upward through the lips and a weight a foot or so above the bait to take it down. They cast this rig over weedy and sandy flats in relatively shallow water, leaving it on the bottom until a smallmouth picks it up.

Striped Bass

Even though schools of striped bass enter coastal rivers (such as the Hudson, Sacramento and San Joaquin) to spawn, and smaller ones often remain year-round, the striper until recent years was considered a saltwater fish. That has changed. The vast majority of anglers know that stripers have been successfully introduced in some large lakes and impoundments. Though they generally don't grow as big as their saltwater cousins, which occasionally weigh 70 pounds or more, freshwater stripers are formidable adversaries on rod and reel, some weighing in the 50- to 60-pound class.

The striped bass is called a "rockfish" or "rock" in Southern areas because its habitat is rocky waters. In the Northeast it has been nicknamed "linesides" due to the eight or so dark longitudinal stripes along its greenish to blackish back and silver sides.

Stripers migrate from lakes up rivers to spawn April through July, depending on region, when water is in the 60- to 67-degree range. They spawn amid boulders and gravel.

Except in spring and fall, the freshwater striper is a deep-water fish although schools may come to the surface in summer in certain areas to feed. When fish aren't showing on top, follow the now-familiar pattern of fishing rocky structure at

Casting With A Button

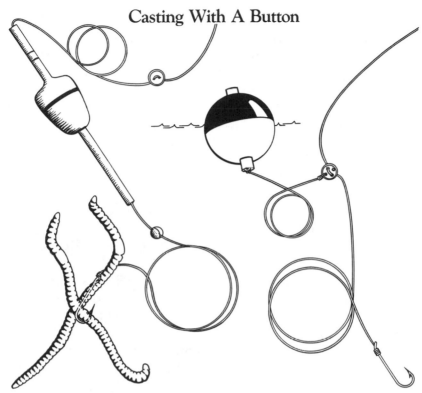

A small button can be used as a sliding stop for fishing a bobber. Float is strung on the line above the split shot for easier casting, but slides up the line to the button when in the water (left). A water-weighted bubble float can be attached to a button with a short piece of monofilament (right). The depth of the bait can be regulated by sliding the button on the line.

the striper's favorite temperature depth. While this may vary somewhat between southern and northern latitudes, it generally is in the vicinity of 63 degrees.

To fish deep for stripers, anglers use the same methods as for lake trout: trolling, jigging or plugging at the correct temperature level along rocky shores, drop-offs and submerged structure, including brush piles. They use downriggers to take plugs, spoons and spinner-and-worm combinations down deep. Stationary fishing calls for dressed or undressed jigs, jig and eel combinations, or live bait such as gizzard shad. Although usually hungry, striped bass can be temperamental at times, so you may have to experiment. Vertical jigging from a drifting boat is a favorite method from spring through fall.

When stripers are feeding on baitfish near the surface,

usually in spring and fall when surface water temperature is right, schools can often be located by observing birds diving to feed on the baitfish themselves. Be ready for action with at least two rods rigged; perhaps one with a surface-popping lure and another with a metal jig like a Hopkins. Since running a boat into the school will put it down, circle it close enough to cast into the edge. If one lure doesn't bring a smashing strike, drop that rod and use the other. There isn't time to rerig, the school will stay near surface only for a few minutes, rarely as long as half an hour. Don't depend entirely on birds to find schools for you. Look for surface commotion.

Spinning or baitcasting tackle, with lines in the 10- to 15-pound-test range, is ideal for this kind of fishing. Lures between 1 and 1½ ounces are needed to get good distance on casts. Fly rods are very sporty but take too much time getting the line out, and winds may make long casts impossible.

In the spring, look for striper schools migrating into river mouths and up the rivers. This is the ideal time for light-tackle angling. Stripers, like largemouths, come into the shallows to feed near dusk and during the night. Try fishing for them on moonlit nights when the fish can be heard, and their swirls can be seen as they feed. Spinning, spincasting or baitcasting tackle is useful, with lines in the 10-pound range, or even lighter in unobstructed water. Surface popping baits and wigglers— Rapalas, Mirro-lures or their imitations—are productive. Fish them slowly, the poppers with a jerky action, the swimmers with a steady retrieve.

White Bass

The striped bass and the white bass are thought to have originally been the same species, the white bass having become landlocked in ages past like salmon. In Southern lakes, schools of them have been seen flurrying to the surface like stripers. At other times, when drifting in shallow, gravely coves, anglers have seen schools of small white bass swimming there. They are fun to fish for because they are finical feeders, swimming behind a lure and carefully inspecting it before they strike. A slight change of action often induces them to take. These little cove fish rarely weigh as much as 4 or 5 pounds, but average 1 to 2 pounds in most areas. They are great sport on ultra-light tackle.

White bass are exciting and exhausting when you hit on a school. You can take them as fast as you can get a line back in the water.

Crappies

The differences between the two species of crappie, black and white, are so slight that they can be generally discussed as a single species.

In the spring—earlier in the South and later in the North—the secret of finding crappies is to locate their spawning areas. These are in rooty or weedy shallows, usually near shore, in water between 1 and 10 feet deep. The best shallows are near drop-offs providing escape to deeper water, where the fish go after spawning.

Before spawning, crappies school in the drop-offs near the shallows, and they remain nearby for a week or two after spawning, so fishing in the shallows and along the drop-offs may be good for a month or more in spring. In deep lakes, the fish never go very deep, preferring depths of 70-degree water. Best fishing in spawning shallows is on the windward shore where winds have driven surface food.

After spawning, loose schools of crappies go to deeper water where there is protective cover, submerged brush piles, stumps and dead trees, and deep channels. Or they seek shade near rocks, bridge abutments and docks. Impoundments, particularly in Southern states, often provide abundant patches of brush piles, their tops usually showing above water. These usually are hotspots, and the biggest fish roam their centers. Thus, lures must be fished into the brush. This isn't as difficult as it might seem, but it does suggest taking along plenty of lures! In Southern areas, water temperatures aren't very critical in shallow lakes because surface and bottom temperatures vary little and the fish are on or near bottom there. Crappies also seek deeper holes with sand or gravel bottoms. Like bass, they seem to shun muddy bottoms.

As spring progresses and warmer weather arrives, crappies, like bass, seek deeper water during the day and may come into the shallows to feed toward dusk. Unlike bass, they do not prefer weedbeds, lily pads or grassy areas, but they do come into other structure which have been mentioned.

The traditional way of fishing for crappies was with a cane pole and a small, live minnow on a thin-wire hook suspended from a bobber to keep it at the desired depth. Spinning tackle usually gets the nod from today's anglers, though long, graphite poles have their fans.

Actually, artificial lures, if fished correctly, can be superior to bait. One of the best is the jig. They come in a variety of sizes between $\frac{1}{32}$ and $\frac{1}{4}$ ounce, and come in a variety of colors and materials. They can be cast over spawning areas or into brush piles or other bottom structure and jigged out slowly. Since the single hook rides upward, a jig doesn't hang up often. When crappies are lying along drop-offs, they can be located by slowly trolling a jig, or perhaps two in tandem, though small crankbaits are becoming more and more popular for this type of fishing. Try different depths to locate the strike zone.

Small weighted spinners are popular here and there, but they are inclined to snag. Since they must be fished slowly, the blade may not revolve. Pork-rind strips are also good crappie

This crappie that weighed in at 1 pound, 10½ ounces fell victim to a jig and minnow combination. The fish was taken from a farm pond.

lures. Light-colored artificials imitating beetles, grubs and minnows, on No. 10 to 6 hooks, with or without small beads and a spinner, often produce. A split shot or two may be needed a foot or so above the lure.

Bluegills

Usually called bream (pronounced "brim") in the South, this tasty, colorful and spunky bluegill is often underrated by anglers who have only hooked small ones in shallow water.

Bluegills are found in brush piles, flooded dead timber and other structure, but, unlike crappies, they are found near or in weedbeds, lily pads and grassy areas. Look for them near drop-offs of shallows with cover, off grassy points of land, and in stream channels.

A nice bluegill like this is a joy to catch. When you find one, there are usually more waiting for the bait.

Also, unlike crappies, bluegills rarely take minnows, although they do consume tiny fry, often of their own kind. Their diet includes insects, crickets, grasshoppers and shrimp. Catalpa worms are a favorite bait for them in the South, and garden worms in the North.

In addition to these baits, bluegills, when feeding near the surface, take deer-hair bugs, sponge-rubber or chenille spiders and tiny poppers. When they're deep, bluegills hit wet flies (such as small Muddler Minnows) night crawlers, small leeches, crickets and tiny jigs, sweetened with a live bait.

Small bluegills build nests in spring in shallow water. The bigger ones make them deeper, usually between 5 and 10 feet, along sandy or gravel shorelines or on shallow reefs. Like bass, they often come into the shallows at dusk to feed, and they retire to the depths when near-surface water is too warm.

Bluegills are very fussy about temperature, preferring water about 73 degrees. Thus, you must experiment with depth, perhaps starting at 4 or 5 feet and going deeper until the strike zone is located. If you are catching small fish, move to a different spot. When you take a big one, you can assume that others should be nearby.

Floats are recommended to keep lures at proper depth and to signal light strikes. When the bobber indicates a strike, hook the fish instantly, before it has time to expel the lure.

Yellow Perch

In the spring when the water exceeds 45 degrees, yellow perch migrate from lakes and ponds up feeder streams to spawn. In some rivers the size of the runs is amazing. Anglers can fill their freezers with tasty fillets by casting small spoons, spinners, jigs or back-hooked minnows beneath a float. Since perch seem to like lures with a bit of yellow in them, a popular bucktail is one with a silver tinsel body and a wing of peacock herl over yellow over white, perhaps with a red throat.

After the spawn, look for perch in shallow coves and over reefs having sandy bottoms with patches of vegetation. They may also be in the shade of breakwaters and docks. Their favorite water temperature is in the 68-degree range, which is often not over 10 feet in depth—although in midsummer they may be much deeper. Serious perch fishermen use their sonar to find the best reefs or mounds.

Baits for perch include worms, crickets, grasshoppers, crayfish, grubs and insects, but their favorite is baitfish about 2 inches long. The usual practice is to first troll a minnow (hooked upward through the lips) with a split shot or two on the line a foot or so above the bait to keep it down. When someone hooks a large perch, the anchor is lowered and trolling gives way to casting. The same rig can still be used, but the minnow should be hooked under the dorsal fin.

Yellow perch are daytime feeders and will take baits or lures at any time, but the hours between noon and darkness seem to be best. Since the fish are notorious bait stealers, it is important to know when to set the hook. On taking the bait, the fish will run with it a short distance before swallowing it. Allow the fish to do this, then set the hook.

=18=

The Pike Family

T he smallest member of the pike family is called the "chain pickerel" because of its chainlike markings. Pickerel inhabit streams, lakes and ponds, principally in the Northeast. Bass fishermen often catch them in bass waters. Lures and tackle are the same as for bass, but a short wire leader, or (preferably) a short length of 10-pound-test monofilament is used. Pickerel have sharp teeth.

Fly-rodders can have fun casting along weedlines with worn bucktails or streamers. Use the old ones you almost threw away; pickerel will strike at almost anything that moves. Flies with Keel hooks or weed guards are needed when casting into holes in grasses and pads.

Northern Pike

Northern pike are found in most of Canada and across the northern United States. Their average weight depends on the waters being fished; 10- and 15-pound fish are large in heavily-fished areas while 20- to 30-pounders are common in many remote Canadian lakes.

Pike are fussy about water temperatures, preferring cool water. When weather is near freezing, they may be in fairly deep water, but they come into weedy shallows in spring to spawn and again return to such places in the winter. They are active during the winter and are taken through the ice, usually over weedbeds 10 to 20 feet deep. During the spring, they are

When you know where to find them, the big pike, such as this 19-pounder caught by a NAFC member, are going to be vulnerable to a well presented offering even if the angler isn't well acquainted with the lake or stream he's fishing.

found in the weedy shallows of bays and coves, usually over weedbeds near the shade of logs, pads and grasses. Their favored areas are near their food supply, which consists of smaller fish, also frogs, small animals and occasionally floating birds. Pike, especially large pike, head for deep water during the warm summer months.

Pike are taken on any tackle suitable for large bass. As a guard against their sharp teeth, use a short wire leader, or one of about 30-pound-test monofilament. I have seen fishermen frustrated in excellent pike areas because they used large spoons which sank too quickly and got caught in weeds. Of course, the trick there is to use large spinnerbaits, floating plugs or shallow divers. The most fun is to use surface poppers and to see pike rise and smash at them. In a good pike area, you only have to

The Pike Family

fancast from a drifting or anchored boat. The speed of retrieve or the action given to the lure can make a tremendous difference, so alternate from slow to fast until you see what produces best.

Muskies

The behemoth of the pike family is the muskellunge, which can weigh 60 pounds or more. A fish a yard long and a bit over 10 pounds is considered a small one in most areas. Muskie country is roughly the states around the Great Lakes, including Canada, but the muskie's range is spreading due to stocking programs. They are now found as far south as the Tennessee Valley.

Fishermen have been known to fish for muskie for several seasons without ever hooking one. On the other hand, there are specialists who catch them regularly. Anglers without experience who want to try the sport should employ a guide, who will know more than can be provided here.

Possessing a seemingly insatiable appetite, the muskie preys on everything that it can catch. In its domain, the muskie will find a hideaway such as the roots of a dead tree, a logjam or a hole in the weeds and only leave in order to find food. Thus a swirl without a take indicates a muskie's abode, which should be marked and fished again.

Muskellunge are primarily fished for in shallow water, but they do suspend over deep water if conditions are right. They spawn in the shallows in spring and only go to deeper water temporarily when the shallows rise above 75 degrees in summer. Sixty-five degrees is good muskie water. This is weedy, brushy or stumpy water in the quiet coves of big rivers; structure near the edges of pools below waterfalls, near rocky ledges, and in weedy, lily-padded bays often congested with stumps and logs. In such places trolling may be impractical, so anglers have to hunt their prey by looking for likely spots in the hope of finding the one among many inhabited by a big fish, and then inducing it to strike.

Casters prospect for muskies somewhat as hunters roam the woods trying to outguess deer. Roaming the shallows, they cast their lures into possible muskie lairs and hope for an explosive strike. As for trolling, you need heavy baitcasting equipment, with long rods having backbone enough to set sharp hooks into bony jaws and to work strong fish away from weeds and roots. Lines should test between 20 and 50 pounds, tipped with a foot or so of metal or monofilament leader testing at least 60 pounds. Muskies have sharp teeth!

Handling hooked northern pike and muskies requires caution. After thrashing around they can be reeled in easily, but don't presume that they have given up. When brought into a boat they begin to thrash again with full vigor, rattling treble-hooked plugs so violently that barbs can impale careless handlers. They also are adept at streaking under the boat and smashing tackle. Keep them out a good distance under strong tension, backing the boat if necessary, until you are sure they are completely played out.

Walleyes

Always delicious to eat and sometimes moody, the sporty walleyed pike is actually a member of the perch family. Its range covers a large part of North America and is growing rapidly as this popular fish is introduced into more and more waters. Walleyes average between 2 and 5 pounds, but thousands of 10-pound-plus fish are caught every year.

Walleyes are bottom-huggers, preferring rock, gravel or sand, but in some lakes they may lie over mud. They will also suspend, and in some lakes such as Lake Erie the best way to catch them is to troll crankbaits behind planer boards.

For years, most anglers thought a walleye's eyes were poorly adapted to bright light conditions, allowing them to inhabit the shallows only at night or when the water is cloudy, the sky overcast or the surface disturbed by waves. This line of thinking has changed as many anglers are finding fantastic walleye action in waters as shallow as 1 foot—even during mid-day in July. So don't limit your fishing efforts only in deep water.

In spring after ice leaves the lakes, and when water temperatures are between 45 and 50 degrees, walleyes enter the shallows of lakes or run up tributary streams to spawn. In lakes, they seek gravel shorelines, usually near sharply sloping or deep drop-offs, where they lay eggs in shallow water, then leave them alone to hatch. They tolerate water between 55 and 70 degrees, but prefer a temperature of around 60.

Walleyes in rivers are found in the edges of currents (particularly below islands), in sand or gravel channels, in deep holes, along rocky ledges and outcropping, near dead trees in water and in the drop-offs below stream mouths.

I once camped in Canada in late spring on a lake beside a stream mouth to fish for brook trout. A French gentleman in the party turned up his nose at broiled brook trout and would take a fly rod rigged with a streamer fly and small spinner and cast across the stream mouth, allowing the fly to sink and then retrieving it slowly. One cast nearly always provided a walleye of 3 pounds or better, which he cooked for his dinner. He maintained that walleyes tasted much better than trout, and some of the other anglers agreed with him.

Other times in walleye country I have caught all I wanted off drop-offs near stream mouths. The trick here was to fish the lure along the bottom. While spring provides the best stream-mouth fishing, this depends on water temperatures, which may be compatible in such places all during the season.

Finding walleyes in lakes, regardless of season, is a matter of locating proper temperature depths and suitable structure. The fish may lie shallow in spring and fall in water of about 60 degrees between 2 to 15 feet deep. This is influenced by light conditions. In summer, this temperature may be between 20 and 40 feet.

Suitable structure in lakes are rocky or gravel bottoms, drop-offs, rocky outcroppings, riprapping, submerged rocky points, bars, ledges and reefs. Among the best, drop-offs leading to shallows where walleyes can come in to feed at night.

Walleyes travel in schools of similar size fish. A good way to locate them is to backtroll slowly over these structures, allowing lures to bounce bottom. Backtrolling allows the transom to act as a buffer and also keeps lines clear of the propeller.

Many types of tackle can be used for walleyes, but my choice is a medium-action spinning rod with line testing between 6 and 8 pounds. A good trolling rig is made by attaching a three-way swivel to the end of the lower swivel. Attach a 3-foot leader to the upper one, with your choice of lure or bait on it. The sinker should be only heavy enough to bounce bottom.

Jigs are one of the most effective lures for walleyes. The

hook may be sweetened with bait. Small, live minnows are popular, as are nightcrawlers and leeches. These are rigged for trolling by using a fine-wire hook and impaling the minnow upward through both lips, the nightcrawler through the collar and the leech lightly through the large sucker. Walleyes often strike very lightly, so fishing with minnows is a bit of a trick. You must learn to feel the difference between the light strike and the sinker bouncing on bottom. When in doubt, treat it as a "take," drop the rodtip to allow the fish to swallow it, then strike hard.

Artificial lures and spoons are used both for trolling and casting. Popular ones include the Rapala, Bomber Long A, Bagley Bang-O-Lure and Lindy Baitfish.

When walleyes are located by trolling, anglers often anchor their boat and cast for the fish. Bait should be fished at proper depth with bobbers. The bait should hang as close to bottom as possible. Minnows, hooked just below the dorsal fin, are effective. Put a split shot on the line a foot or so above the bait to keep it down. Other good baits are worms, nightcrawlers, leeches, hellgrammites, crayfish and even small frogs.

19

Finding Trout

Y
ears ago, at the start of the New England trout season, I would be up before dawn to be rigged and ready to go at first light. I don't do it any more because it doesn't make much sense. The fact that it's uncomfortably cold and that mush-ice clogs rod guides isn't the main point. The point is that fishing is better in the afternoon when waters get a bit warmer. On a sunny early-season day, water temperatures can rise 15 degrees between sunup and mid-afternoon, and this can make a big difference in the fishing.

Those who want to venture forth when water temperatures are 50 degrees or less are advised to use bait. Bright red garden worms, cleansed of their loam by a day or so in damp moss, more wiggly and less slimy then, are the favorite bait for frigid streams. Hellgrammites, crayfish, grubs, if you can find them, also produce. Add a split shot or two to get them down, if necessary, because the bait should be rolled along the bottom. Some fishermen prefer big nightcrawlers at such times, perhaps on the theory that, if a small worm is good, a bigger one is better. I don't think this is so. Trout adapt their body temperature to that of the surrounding water. When it's cold their metabolism is very low. They hug bottom; won't move to any extent to take food; need very little, and prefer smaller baits to bigger ones.

Many anglers don't enjoy baitfishing for trout, but it seems to be the best answer in cold weather. Those who want to use

Satisfaction is evident in this angler's face as a nice 2-pound brown trout surfaces and comes toward the angler's net.

Finding Trout   219

flies early in the season can try nymphs, small streamers or bucktails, fished slowly on the bottom. Small spinners or spoons, worked as slowly as possible along the bottom, also are good bets. Some fishermen who "sweeten" their streamers or hardware by adding a piece of worm to the hook. If it's fresh, it may add the enticement of scent.

Another aversion is to fish for freshly stocked hatchery trout, most of which are dumped into streams in early season to make fishermen feel their licenses are good investments. Tame trout expect to be fed, and will take almost anything that moves. A fisherman phoned one day to report taking his limit in a few minutes. He theorized that, since hatchery trout were fed liver, they must have grown fond of it. So he obtained a piece of beef liver, cut it into strips, and baited his hook by impaling the end of a strip on the barb. He said it had worms beaten seven ways to Sunday!

With that, let a few weeks pass and discuss trout fishing when the weather is more comfortable.

On a day later in spring I took water temperatures hourly while fishing with nymphs and small streamers. At 9 a.m. the stream's temperature was 51 degrees, and was only a degree warmer at 10. It had raised 4 degrees to 55 by 11, and 3 more at noon to 58. The morning's fishing was poor; mostly small ones. By one o'clock, the stream had warmed 2 more degrees to 60; then a big jump to 64 an hour later. This rise to ideal temperature levels brought a decided improvement in the fishing. Fish that had hugged bottom in the colder water now began to rise. The warmth brought on a small insect hatch, causing dimples and splashes in holding spots behind midstream rocks and along steep, brushy banks. Conditions like this make flies and weighted lures superior to bait. One reason is that you can keep them fishing. Bait must be changed frequently. When you're fussing with bait, you're taking time away from fishing!

Anglers who take stream temperatures can tell whether they should fish along the bottom or higher up. They can predict when trout should leave holding areas and travel to feeding ones such as riffles and the tails of pools. They can accurately guess what types of lures or flies to use.

The holding spots of trout in rivers and streams have been discussed in previous chapters. The pattern of brown trout differs slightly from that of the other stream trout. Browns can tolerate somewhat warmer water, up to 75 degrees or so, if it contains enough oxygen. They prefer places where they can remain hidden, such as the dark waters of undercut streambanks, culverts with moderate or slowly flowing water, and the sanctuaries provided by tree roots and logjams. Look for the big ones in the more inaccessible spots.

Brown trout are also fonder of night feeding than brookies and rainbows seem to be. Find a good brown trout pool and become familiar with it during daylight. Plan how you would fish the pool after dark. Then, go there by moonlight and fish for the big ones, which should be venturing from their hideaways. Brown trout seem to lose much of their caution after dark, and they look for food by sound as well as by sight and scent. Frogs that make too much commotion don't last very long. Big floating flies and sinking streamers, slapped on the surface, may bring strikes.

Brown trout have a well-deserved reputation for being smart, and they are smart enough to know when they are safe. A stream flowing through a New York town maintains a protected area for them which doubles as a tourist attraction. People collect on the bridge to watch trophy tackle busters lying peacefully in plain sight in the shallow stream below. The fish lie in the shadow thrown by the bridge, many of them with their noses almost touching the line of sunlight. People feed them, but the town constable lingers nearby to be sure nothing is dropped that has a hook in it. Wherever fishing is allowed, don't neglect the shade under bridges!

Ponds And Lakes

Early in the season, surface fishing is excellent when the ice melts, but only if it has been windy enough to mix the water. Trout and salmon are cold then, and search for relative warmth. Under such conditions you should find them in sunny, shallow water close to the shoreline, where they can find protection under tree roots and fallen timber.

When a good breeze is stirring on a warm day, it pushes warmer surface water to the windward shore, sort of piling it up there. The breeze also carries surface foods. Such an area should most likely be productive.

When buds begin to pop in early spring, the smelt in lakes, as well as some species of baitfish, collect in stream estuaries and move up the streams to spawn. Trout and landlocked salmon know this, and collect near the stream mouths. After spawning, the smelt and baitfish return to the lakes again, so stream mouths should offer excellent spring fishing as long as this period lasts.

The trick is to anchor the boat about 100 feet from the entering stream, over a channel or deep hole, if there is one. Use a streamer fly or bucktail that resembles the baitfish in size and color. Cast it far out on a sinking line, giving it plenty of time to sink deep. Then strip the fly in fast. As it nears the boat, change its action to sharp jerks. Fish may be following the fly and may take it only when it is given different action close to the boat. With this method, the area should be fancasted, and this can be repeated for as long as is desired, because you are working on cruising fish. A fruitless cast to one spot does not mean there won't be a big trout or salmon there on your next cast.

In many places, this kind of fishing is best as early as anglers can pry themselves out of bed. This may be because major baitfish runs happen during the night and just before sunrise, or because the gamefish feed more actively then.

Of course, an alternative to casting is trolling; close to the surface when water temperatures are correct, but deeper when necessary. Fly-rodders using streamers or bucktails should let out 50 feet or so of sinking line, and give the fly, which is only slightly below the surface, a bucktailing action. If this doesn't work, add a split-shot or two to the leader butt. Color-coded lead-cored lines are the alternative for going deeper. Long, bright wobblers or small lures are used for deep trolling.

After most of the baitfish have left the streams, schools may be found in the lake or traveling near shore. These schools are usually followed by the trout and landlocked salmon.

Summer Trout Fishing

As surface waters grow warmer, to 65 degrees or more, the spring pattern changes to a more or less static one which lasts until the cold weather of fall. Let's see where to find fish under these circumstances.

Temperature-Activity Table For Trout

Water Surface Temperatures	Water Temperature	Fish Action	Fishing Status	Fish Location	Suggested Lures
freezing to 40°F	much too cold	inactive	very poor	very deep (in lakes or pools)	bait fished deep
40°-50°F	too cold	passive	fair	deep (Or along shorelines or riffles where water is warmer)	live bait spoons or spinners nymphs streamer flies
50°-60°F	just right	active	good	near surface	wet flies streamer flies nymphs spoons or spinners
60°-70°F	just right	very active	excellent	near surface	dry or wet flies streamer flies nymphs spoons or spinners
70°-80°F	too warm*	active to passive	fair	deep (Or in spring holes, brook mouths, shaded streams)	live bait streamer flies nymphs spoons or spinners
80°F and up	much too warm	inactive	very poor	very deep (Or in spring holes and cold water brooks)	bait fished deep

(to the left of the table, bracketing the rows:) Tolerant Temperatures | Optimum Temperatures

(Copyright 1949, 1971 and 1974 by Joseph D. Bates, Jr.)

Bates used a scientific approach to fishing. He developed this chart for trout as a guide for neophyte fishermen. Bates acknowledged that these temperature ranges were more accurate for brook trout than for rainbows or browns which remain active in warmer water.

When the air is colder than the water, the fishing should be poor, and there should be no surface activity. Fog over the water usually indicates this. You have the choice of working the bottom or of waiting until the sun warms the air. This is also true of windy days, because there are fewer hatches then, and those that occur are driven from the stream.

Conversely, summer fishing should be good during or after a rain, particularly when the river is rising. While this may discolor the stream a bit, it also dislodges food, washing it downstream and putting trout on the feed. I remember many instances of this. My fishing companion dropped me off at a bridge about a mile and a half downstream from where he would fish. Soon after he left, a pelting rain began, but since there was no cover, I continued fishing. Nearly every time I cast the tiny streamer fly to a good-looking spot a trout took it. Many of them were surprisingly large. I switched to nymphs, with the same result. Fish were on the feed and took almost anything. I released all but two, which were enough for dinner. At dusk, I arrived at the lower bridge and found my partner asleep in the car. He had done poorly because he hadn't wanted to get wet!

When streams are warm in summer, look for places that cool them, and carefully fish for trout there. Cold-water brooks are excellent places because trout collect at their mouths and they run up them in summer. If the bank is undercut where the brook enters the stream, the mouth is almost sure to be a hotspot. When the stream is too warm, try the brook itself.

Another sign of a hotspot is trickling cold water from a spring. Such trickles often come from a gravel bank, or as tiny brooklets flowing in. Look for protection where they enter the stream, or slightly downstream of it.

Anglers who watch water temperatures look for signs of feeding activity when these temperatures are optimum for trout. Part of their education is to sit quietly on a bank and to look into a pool to see what's going on.

Ponds And Lakes

A knowledge of water temperatures is important in finding trout in ponds and lakes during the summer. We may see trout, or put lures near them, when temperatures are out of their range (perhaps because they can't find better ones), but they are much less inclined to take lures then. Shoal water is probably too warm, except perhaps early in the morning or late in the evening. Anglers who don't want to fish deep for trout in summer can often find them near the surface in cooler water—the mouths of cold-water brooks and spring holes.

When a breeze is blowing toward an inlet stream, it brings surface foods with it, particularly in summer. The breeze tends to push the foods into the stream mouth, but the stream's current tries to push them back. This causes the formation of a food line. When there is little wind, the line may be scattered and fairly far out, but a stronger wind will compact it and drive it in toward the current. Beginners may not notice this because the line is often rather scummy, and you must look closely to see spent insects and terrestrials in it. If you do look closely you may see the dimples of feeding fish as they suck in these foods from below. In this case, put on a dry or wet fly that approximates the majority of the food, cast it into or near the food line, and give it the slightest possible action to attract attention. A representation of a bee or a grasshopper is excellent.

Another very important type of hotspot in summer is the spring hole. Some of these are deep in pond or lake and can't be found except by luck with a depth thermometer. Once found, their locations should be marked carefully and kept secret, because in summer they will be good year after year.

When near-surface water isn't too warm for feeding activity on ponds and lakes, there are other visible manifestations of where to find fish in addition to the others already discussed. One of these is wind ripples.

Trout (and other fish) which are surface feeding lie below the edges of wind ripples for two reasons. These ripples (or "riffles," as they are sometimes called) give trout more of a feeling of security than do the glassy parts of the lake's surface. For example, during a large midge hatch, the newly hatched chironomids were piling up in windrows at the edge of the ripples, and trout were sucking them in. At other times slight breezes would blow other types of insects to such places.

Another place to find trout when there are no surface or visible subsurface indications of their presence is in a small pond with a weedy bottom. When the surface is very weedy, the trick is to fish open places amid the weeds.

Many lakes have no weeds or pads showing. Then, you have to anchor at random and fancast the area with as long a line as possible. Use a sinking line and work a streamer fly just over the weeds. Give the cast time to sink, counting seconds. You'll bring back grass on some casts, but try to get as deep as possible without doing so. When the fly has had time to sink, it should be stripped fast.

I know of ponds like this in the Northeast where the bottom is so weed-covered that it looks like a dark green rug. All the weeds are about the same height, several feet below the surface. Other such places show more readable structure such as boulders, gravel bars, submerged tree trunks and submerged brush piles. If the lake contains trout, surface-feeding fish will

Fishing A Stream Mouth

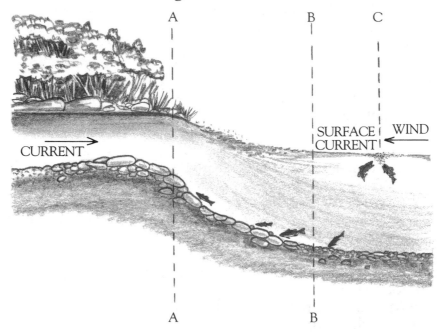

When fishing a stream mouth, shown here from the top, stay well beyond the riffle in order to cast to the drop-off. If there is a breeze blowing toward the mouth, a food line may form against the outflowing current where baitfish and gamefish gather, so anchor farther out and cast to the line.

frequently be observed dimpling, making head-and-tail rises, or swirling along the edges of wind riffles where floating food tends to collect.

When surface water is a bit too warm or cold for trout, they may feed on the surface anyway when a good hatch is in progress. When water is a bit too cold, peak feeding on sunny days should be around noon or early in the afternoon. When water is a bit too warm, the best fishing should be near evening when temperatures start to decline. On cloudy or rainy days, when the light is poor, fish will venture from hiding places more often, making feeding periods longer.

Fall Trout Fishing

When stream temperatures descend toward the low 60s

226   Complete Angler's Library

brook trout and brown trout (as well as landlocked salmon and some other species) move into stream outlets (often as far out as stream currents exist) to wait until water temperature, volume of flow and the urgency to spawn impel them to swim upstream, sometimes far up into the gravel of small feeder brooks. In Maine's former wilderness, I have parted streamside bushes after the fishing season closed in October and have seen so many brook trout lying over the gravel that nearly all of the stream's bottom was covered by them. Brown trout do this, too, spawning in some areas as late as February. Both species also will spawn in shallow gravel or rocky areas of lakes if satisfactory stream conditions do not exist.

Thus, in the fall, the places to fish are outlets of streams flowing into lakes. Look for fairly deep channels with moderate flow, particularly in the shade. Such places may be quite wide. Perhaps believing in the safety of numbers, the fish are less shy than usual, but they may not take lures as avidly as their urge to spawn increases.

This is a time to take trophy trout. Many big ones, which now grace the walls of sportsmen, were caught quite easily and without much skill because so many were concentrated near stream mouths or farther upstream in pools and runs. To avoid having too many taken, and thus to help preserve the fishery, many states close their trout seasons before spawning reaches its peak, but the legal week or two before this can provide fabulous fishing. In this age when trouting needs all the help it can get, anglers are urged to use restraint by fishing for fun and limiting the kill to a single trophy, if any at all. Of course, the trophy should be a male. Males are more colorful for mounting, and not as necessary for reproductive purposes because one can fertilize the eggs of several females.

Ponds And Lakes

When cold fall nights reduce surface temperatures of lakes, the trout begin to roam more widely. The solutions to finding them depend on water temperatures and structure; this being stream mouths (which we have discussed), logjams, rocky coves, windward shores and other various places which now should be familiar.

It pays to be observant. One day a French-Canadian guide

and I were fishing a remote lake in northern Quebec. In outboarding from one spot to another, I noticed a shady cove filled with drifted logs, and called the guide's attention to it. He shook his head. "No fish there," he said.

After supper I took a canoe and went there alone. The water was clear and deep, and the setting sun threw shadows over the cove. I quietly drifted in until the canoe sidled up to a floating log, put a streamer fly into the air, and dropped it near a log. There was an immediate swirl, and a big trout had it. He bored down deeply. The trick, of course, was to try to get him away from the logjam, which I managed somehow or other by backing the canoe with a paddle in one hand while holding the fly rod in the other.

Out in deeper water it was necessary to use all the power the leader's tip would stand to prevent the fish from snagging on dead branches which littered the bottom. The trout stayed near the surface and I finally netted him. He was a fat, humpbacked male brook trout weighing 6¼ pounds and brilliant in his fall mating colors.

After gloating over this prize, I drifted in again and cast the same streamer to another log. A cast or two later hooked another male trout of almost the same size. I brought him to boat, removed the fly from his jaw, and watched him swim away, perhaps to give another angler a thrill at another time.

The trout saved was mounted. He looks down from the wall as I write this; a reminder that it pays to know how to "read the water" and to use one's own judgment. The spot may have been a spawning area. I don't know. By the time the second fish was released it was too dark to try any more, and the aircraft came in for us the next morning.

Index

Plastic worms, 35, 82, 202
Ploppers, 148
Plunkers, 148
Points, 76, 80-82, 97, 127
Polarized sunglasses, 84, 110, 160
Ponds, 22, 40, 45, 86-87, 221-222, 224-226
Pools, 101-103, 114-118
Popper bugs, 90
Poppers (lures), 34, 152, 179
Propbaits, 152
Propeller blade, 155

R
Rainbow trout, 25, 40, 90
Rattlers, 148
Rattling lures, 34, 148
Reading water, 14
Reefs, 84-85
Reservoirs, 79
Riffles, 99-101, 176
Rip jigging, 136, 142-146
Rivers, 40, 92-113
Roach, Gary, 56-58
Rockfish, 204
Rocks, 115-116
Rock-fill structure, 88-89
Runs, 105, 111

S
Salmon, 26, 107-108
Salmon eggs, 190
Schuett, Mike, 76
Senses, 26-35
Shade, 113
Shallow-water jigs, 138-139
Shallows, 86-87, 180, 202
Shore fishing, 77
Sight, 26-30
Slip floats, 146-147
Slip-sinker rigs, 145
Smallmouth bass, 83, 84, 86, 98, 157, 171, 192, 198, 202-204
Smell (sense of), 34-35
Smelt, 25
Sonar, 14, 51, 58-68, 80, 130-132
Sonar sensitivity, 59-63, 64

Sonic lures, 32
Sosin, Mark, 26
Sound, 30
Spawning, 23, 24, 25, 198-200, 203
    locations, 23, 198
    migrations, 24-25
    seasons, 23
    species information, 23
    water temperature, 23
Speed-jigging, 138, 163
Spincasting reels, 186-188, 190
Spinnerbaits, 82, 202
Spinners, 32-33, 83, 98, 116, 118, 154-157
Spinning reels, 186-188, 190
Splashers (lures), 34, 148
Splaywings, 172
Splutters, 148
Spoon weight, 160, 162
Spoons, 82, 83, 98, 116, 158-165
Spotlights, 70
Spring turnover, 43
Standing timber, 89-90
Steelhead, 99, 107-108, 109, 111
Steep banks, 103-104
Stickbaits, 153
Stillfishing, 44
Stone flies, 204
Streambeds, 78-80, 118
Streamers, 83, 90, 98, 103, 118, 166-172, 202
Streams, 20, 24-25, 38, 114-123, 156
Strike zones, 53
Striped bass, 34, 157, 204-206
Structure, 20, 22, 48, 50-52, 76-77, 78-91
Structure fishing, 78
Submerged boulders, 102-103, 117
Submerged islands, 84-86
Submerged roadbeds, 87-88
Sufficient oxygen requirement, 22
Sunfish, 36
Suppression controls (sonar), 63
Surface lures, 28, 33-34, 45, 82, 148, 151-153, 202
Surface markers, 85-86
Suspended fish, 48, 51, 128, 134
Swimmers, 148

Swing retrieve, 170-171

T

Temperature gauges, 68-69
Texas-rigged plastic worm, 160
Thermocline level, 40, 44, 45, 69
Thermometers, 39-40, 44
Thoroughfares, 83
Time of day, 117, 179
Tip-ups, 128
Transducer, 59, 60, 131
Trolling, 51, 162
Trolling lures, 150-151
Trolling speed indicators, 69
Trout, 22, 34-35, 36, 38, 45, 69, 80,
  92-113, 114-123, 157, 218-228

U

Undercut river banks, 119

V

Vegetation, 22
Vertical lures, 163
Vibrating baits, 150
Video display sonar, 59

W

Wading, 27, 86
Walleyes, 36, 84, 90, 157, 192, 215-217
Walton, Izaak, 182, 186

Water clarity, 24, 49-50, 144, 156
Water density, 40
Water depth, 22, 39, 43, 50
Water flow, 20
Water temperature, 17-18, 19, 24, 25,
  29-30, 36-45, 50, 68, 80, 82, 86, 99,
  128, 198, 202, 203, 204, 211, 212
Water turbidity, 201
Waterfalls, 114-115
Weather, 53, 107-108, 117, 138
Weedless spoons, 160
Weedless bucktails, 168-170
Weedless streamers, 168-170
Weeds, 86-87, 106
Weighted bucktails, 170
Weighted streamers, 170
Weight-forward spinners, 157
Welch, Herbie, 15-16
Wet flies, 172-173
White bass, 157, 206
Willowleaf blade, 154
Wind, 42, 82
Wind jigging, 139-141
Wobblers, 148
Worms, 188, 204

Y

Yellow perch, 24-25, 211